WOMEN HOME, EXCELLED MEN

WOMEN HOME, EXCELLED MEN
Essays to Enliven You

HEMALATHA GNANASEKAR

KALPAZ

Women Home, Excelled Men : Essays to Enliven You

Rs. 540

ISBN: 978-81-7835-726-3

Published in 2009 in India by
Kalpaz Publications
C-30, Satyawati Nagar,
Delhi-110052
Phone : 9212729499
E-mail: kalpaz@hotmail.com

Lasser Type Setting by: Rudra Computer Graphics, Delhi
Printed at : G. Print Process, Delhi

This is dedicated to Shirdi Sai Baba, whose blessings enabled me to write this book

Contents

Preface

Growing up as a girl was tough three decades ago! It was the time when parents thought twice before sending a girl child to one of the best schools. For they believed that a girl belonged to her husband's family. She was also brought up in a very conservative environment; so much so that, talking to a stranger or relatives was considered a taboo. Friends were not allowed and laughing aloud or embellishing oneself were also forbidden.

In my book "Women Home Excellent Men" I have recorded my experience of growing up in such a background. Today, if I sit down and think about my past, all I would like to say is that: despite the restraints, life was really enjoyable. There were no televisions for entertaining us nor were we familiar with the computer which would connect us to the outside world. All the fun I got was through books, which I slowly got addicted to. There were a few people who influenced my life, and through close observance, I learnt some lessons from them, which I follow to this day!

Our family doctor taught me to accept life as it comes, without any fretting and fuming. From an old school teacher, I learnt that it is love that triumphs over everything and ultimately stopped worrying about ageing. I also learnt the lesson that the value of money is enhanced, if only it is spent for others and to see the smile on their face. And at times, I also wonder at how crazy I had been as a child, when all I was determined to do in life was speak the truth, no matter what!

While you may perhaps have a hearty laugh reading them, I am sure you would not miss out on the fact that life offers lessons to each one of us from time to time and if only, we care to stand-by and take note of them, we would find our lives enriched!

Truly enlivening, these essays are chicken soup for your soul!

2009 **Hemelatha Gnanasekar**

1

Sublime Feat

It was a very small gathering of devout people. All around there was unusual silence and the children also were watching the action avidly. The pujari was performing abhishekam to the Goddess in the sanctum. First, he poured a bucketful of milk over the Goddess, followed by a thick paste of sandalwood and a pot full of water. Again, he took a basket of mixed fruits and offered it to the Goddess. Finally, he rinsed everything off with water brought from the stream flowing near the temple.

The abhishekam complete, he began to embellish the Goddess with a beautiful silk cloth and bedecked her with kumkum and flowers. Then, he performed arti with burning camphor in front of the Goddess, while the congregation chanted prayers which sanctified the atmosphere. Some of the people gathered there explained the powers of the Goddess to those who were not aware of it, speaking in hushed tones.

An old woman advised her granddaughter to pray to the Goddess with folded palms, when all of a sudden, the child enquired aloud, "But where is the Goddess ?" The question put forth by the little girl, induced laughter and the serious mood which prevailed turned to a jovial and relaxed one.

This was the first time I was visiting the temple and my mind was also occupied with the very same question that the child had candidly asked. For all that was to be seen there, were three black stone pillars, for which all the elaborate rituals were performed. And I waited eagerly for Grandma to clarify the doubts of the little girl. But Grandma only chided the girl for her outspokenness and threatened her that such questions would arouse the wrath of the Goddess and she would pierce her eyes with a long spear. Immediately, I closed my eyes and mumbled a prayer. I was rather impressed by the love and devotion the people bestowed on a mere black stone pillar revering it as a powerful Goddess. It showed the intensity of faith people have in God!

The fear of God has been inculcated in me since childhood. I had been taught that God is present in each and every speck of the universe and that He is Omnipresent, Omniscient and Omnipotent! Though I believe in this concept of God, there is a slight variation in my conviction. I see God only in those people who come to rescue me or help me out in times of danger or distress and trust they are sent by God. To some extent, I am of the opinion that God exists in the people around us. But to consider His presence in an inanimate thing as a stone or tiny particle is beyond my comprehension.

I was thus reminded instantly of a man whom I had come across during my school days. When the assembly prayer was being sung, he would pass by the road carrying a bag in each hand. It was his time for shopping and his bags would be full of vegetables or provisions. After walking a few paces, he would put his bags down. Folding his palms together, he would mumble a prayer to the Sun God, looking up at the sky. Then, after humbly bowing down, he would continue walking. After a couple of minutes he would repeat the same actions.

We had strict instructions to close our eyes while singing the school prayer. On days, when there was no teacher spying nearby, out of curiosity, I would try and peek to count the number of times that man stopped to offer his prayers to the Sun God, until he disappeared out of view. After seeing the vehement faith that the people bestowed on a mere black stone pillar, my opinion that he was insane, changed altogether. May be this man revered his God to a great extent, and he saw Him in the form of the Sun!

Once, while I was on my way to my sister's place, I saw a large crowd gathered on both sides of the road and our car could not proceed further. One of them told us that the road was closed for another one hour as a religious procession was to pass by in a short while. After parking our vehicle, we decided to join them. Had it been any political procession, I would have asked my hubby to take a different route, but since it was a religious one, I waited to see it. It had been a long time since I had witnessed such a religious procession.

During the summer vacations we would go to our grandfather's village. There were many temples there and religious processions were quite a common affair. The God or Goddess of different temples would be taken out in a procession. There were special carts meant to carry the statues of the Gods. Generally, when the procession reached Grandpa's house, it would halt for a considerable time, and we would offer flowers, coconuts and fruits to the pujari and a special puja would be performed for us. Then as the bullock cart moved on, a small band would follow, playing the drums and singing bhajans. This would be then followed by a troop of men wearing masks of horses and walking tall with false horse feet, or dancing all the way accompanied by the bursting of crackers.

Stages would be set-up near the temples for enactment of dramas, usually scenes from the epics of the Ramayana and

Mahabharata. Though I would understand nothing of the epics, we children would keep lingering around the temple throughout the day, admiring the actors and actresses doing their make-up. At midnight, when the drama began, people would squat on the vast stretch of sand and watch with keen interest.

After Grandpa passed away, our trips to the village also stopped. Since then, I had missed the joys of participating in a religious congregation.

Now looking around, I found the same kind of excitement in the air. People from far off places had come all the way to witness the procession and they were thrilled to be there and waited with bated breath to see the procession pass through. Seeing the joyous and gay mood prevailing all around, I became all the more inquisitive to know more about the kind of procession that was to pass by.

Suddenly, the crowd stilled and an air of expectation filled the air as everyone's attention was turned to the procession visible at the corner of the road. As the procession slowly moved closer, I was enthralled by the spectacular scene that I saw.

The first to emerge in the sequence was an autorickshaw towed by a young boy of twelve. A small incision had been made on his back below the nape, and an iron hook had been inserted through the slit. A thick rope was tethered to the hook and was connected to the auto. Also, a sharp metal spear passed through his perforated tongue. He tugged the auto slowly, steadily and effortlessly. There was no hint of pain on his face and he was accompanied by his family members, who trotted beside him, chanting the name of their beloved Goddess. This was followed by several other autos, towed by different men, single-handedly. Some of the autos carried people too, and they were all effortlessly hauled leaving the onlookers spellbound.

In a short while, we were to observe an even more horrific scene. It was the towing of lorries. Each lorry way pulled by three men, with the help of thick ropes, secured to hooks on their backs. At the four corners of the open lorry, pillars were erected and a temporary ceiling – a framework of metal bars – was fabricated. On these metal rods were fixed a number of hooks from which metal chains dangled. These metal chains were fastened to the hooks embedded in the bodies of the men who hung vertically, horizontally and upside down from the framework of the metal bars. In some of these lorries the relatives of these men were seated, applauding and inspiring them!

The sight of the hooks tearing into the flesh, left me horrified. In one particular lorry, a man, hanging horizontally from the metal bars, with face down, had a cradle bound to the hooks on his chest and a few onlookers got their newborns blessed by placing them in it. It was a sight that sent a shiver through my body and also moved me to tears.

This unique procession continued for more than an hour and we stood there agape, beholding the sublime feat of these strong-willed men, unmindful of the passing of time.

Surely, some miraculous power must be sustaining them, during this ordeal!

This deed, beyond doubt, was the culmination of love and reverence towards their goddess exhibited in the most weird form, and it left an indelible impression on our minds.

This stupendous act of piercing and slitting of their flesh to glorify their goddess, shows the sublime heights that man can transcend to get nearer to God. Undoubtedly, an atheist viewing the spectacle, would have second thoughts on the concept of God and certainly change his mind!

2

The Exotic Van Journey

It was one hour past the scheduled time and our legs were beginning to ache, as we waited with bated breath for the van to arrive. At last, one of us caught a glimpse of an apple-green van at the corner of the street. Suddenly, the air was filled with excitement and the children squealed with joy. When the green van stopped near our house, all of us scrambled into it. Though it was twelve-seater, twenty of us squeezed in, with children sitting on our laps.

The occasion was the ear-piercing ceremony of my one-year-old daughter. It is the custom in our family that the first head-tonsuring and ear-piercing should be carried out in the temple of our family Goddess, which was situated in some remote corner of the village. Comfortably settled, we got ready for the gala picnic. The festive mood infected even the old grandparents who were delighted to be going to the sanctum of their family goddess, after a very long time.

The van was an eye-sore! It was an ill-kept antique van and was rusted in many parts. Whenever we leaned back, our clothes got stained with rust. The driver was a grumpy old man and when we questioned him regarding the condition of the van, he did not bother to answer and continued to drive the van in a very lethargic and careless manner. As he drove along, the engine produced an odd and deafening sound and this made the horn redundant and kept the other vehicles at bay.

An elderly relative, was narrating his past-stories of riding on bullock carts - and the children listened with rapt attention. He was telling them about his courageous act when once, one of his bulls had taken off. He recounted in detail the dauntless stunts he performed to bring the ox under control. The Children pestered him with a volley of questions and he answered them patiently. Sitting close to him, I was also forced to listen to his never-ending tale. Later, my concentration was interrupted by my husband who said, "the old man sounds so enthusiastic, one would think, he had driven a Benz !" Just then, our van bounced over the rutted road and I replied, "it is no wonder that, travelling in such a van should bring back such memories".

We reached Kanchipuram exactly at noon. From there, we had to travel another 20 Km, to reach the temple of our family goddess. All of us were coming to this place after a pretty long time, and no one was able to give right directions to the driver. A young boy was riding in front of us and we requested our driver to stop the van, so that we could ask for directions. The driver immediately applied his brakes, but the brakes did not oblige him. We held our breath fearing what would happen next. Much to our relief, the driver at last succeeded in stopping the van. But by then, the boy had disappeared from the scene. However, we were satisfied that the brakes did work afterall! We stopped beside a group of villagers who told us which route we had to take.

One of our relatives, who lived in the vicinity of the temple, had been intimated well in advance about our programme. The family received us with a lot of warmth. I was in fact meeting them for the first time. They had made all the arrangements for the head-tonsuring ceremony and had kept the temple priest apprised of our arrival.

While her hair was being cut my daughter cried a lot. The uncles and aunts tried to calm her by showing her new toys and diverting her attention. But she paid no attention to them and continued her loud wailing. Even after the tonsuring and ear-piercing was over, she cried for a very long time. Not having the heart to see my child weeping, I kept myself away from the scene. Finally, when it was over, I lifted her into my arms and cuddled her. She still continued sobbing, until I took her to the van and told her that we were going to return home in a short while and she suddenly burst into laughter. She probably enjoyed the bouncy ride in the old van!

The hall where food was to be served was a very large one, stretching from one end of the street to the other. People squatted on the floor and reminisced about the past. Feeling out of place, I strolled through the huge rooms gaping at the beautiful wall paintings and designs on the ceiling. I stood near the spacious kitchen, marvelling all the while at its enormity, very unlike the kitchens in cities which were so tiny that only one person could stand and cook. Then I popped my head in and saw the women busy cooking. I was full of praise for the village women who had consented to prepare meals at home for such a large gathering, without any fretting. I felt ashamed of myself for ordering meals from a hotel on several occasions, even for a small number of people as I hardly had any confidence in my cooking! The aroma of the curries tickled my senses and increased my appetite. The food was very delicious indeed and I savoured the sumptuous meal. It would be a long time before I would get another opportunity to eat a home-cooked meal.

It was now time for the journey back home. With our tummies full, most of us fell asleep instantly, the jarring sound of the van lulling even the unruly children to sleep. I had a good nap for about an hour. When I opened my eyes, I found everyone around me fast asleep.

Unfortunately, their sleep was disturbed shortly, when all of a sudden, the van came to an abrupt halt. The driver tampered with every possible gadget visible in front of him but the van would not budge an inch. He then turned back and informed us meekly that we had run out of diesel. Whenever my husband was asleep, I would always be extra careful not to disturb him as it would make him mad. However, now he was woken by the clamour around and on learning its cause, gritted his teeth and started screaming at the driver. The place where we were stranded was an isolated and secluded spot, far away from human population.

My imagination ran riot...*The gruff old driver would pull out a gun from out of the blue and pointing it toward us, demand that we part with our jewellery, and he would sell our jewellery and earn an income to last his lifetime for all of us were decked up and wearing expensive jewellery. And I would advise the people to hand over their jewellery without any commotion so that our lives would be saved ...*

All at once, I snapped out of these wild imaginings and nudged my husband, cautioning him to stop cursing and immediately arrange for some diesel.

Ten minutes elapsed but it seemed like ages. Then closing my eyes I mumbled a prayer to God seeking His help. In a short while my prayers were answered. We saw a man riding a bicycle and when he came abreast of us, all of us surrounded him, hounding him with questions about where we could get fuel. He told us that the nearest petrol pump was 5 Km away and readily offered to help us by taking the driver there.

There were trees on both sides of the road. The youngsters climbed the trees and we sprawled on the lush green grass under a shady banyan tree and enjoyed the cool breeze. Finding no one around, my brother, who was in his early teens, tried his hand at the wheel, blowing the horn ceaselessly. He fancied himself to be an ace driver... *He was now speeding in a car on a racetrack, racing ahead of everyone and was at last declared the winner! Overwhelmed with pride he got up from the seat to share the joy of his triumph with everybody...*

His dreams were shattered when all of a sudden the seat gave in and he tumbled out. He lifted the seat and carried it to the banyan tree. Depositing it there, he sat on it and relaxed for a while, tired after the great ordeal. Thereafter each of the children took turns rejoicing on the "throne" and many posed for a photo sitting on it!

My throat was parched and I felt an acute need of water. By now, the water cans were almost empty and lifting a bottle in which there was very little water I began gulping it down, when all of a sudden, I heard a sound like thunder. It was my husband yelling at me to stop drinking the water. He told me that he had saved it, in case our driver needed water for the radiator. For once, I appreciated his prudence and heeded his command.

After an hour our driver returned and we thanked the bicycle man–our godfather–for his timely succour, by rewarding him with cash. He accepted the money with joy writ large on his face, and continued his journey and so did we. The van started off without any problem, and the roaring sound of the van forced us to keep silent. Gradually, the places began to look familiar and I was happy that at last we were going to reach home. That very instant, the van came to a sudden stop. *Not again!* I almost shrieked. It was my husband who had arranged for this van and I was afraid that the others were going to tear him to pieces. I wondered what the driver was up to and felt much relieved when I saw him walk a few yards to attend to nature's call. But my happiness was short-lived, for when the driver tried to start his van, it would not oblige. The driver then explained that the battery was rather weak and if some of us helped him by pushing the van for a short distance, it would immediately start. All of us got down, and the men shoved the van with all their might and the engine roared once again. For a change, now the blaring sound of the engine was pleasant to the ears and hastily we all clambered into the van before it would come to a stop again.

On reaching home, I berated my husband for arranging such a rotten van, who, in turn, lashed out at the cab owner. The cab man listened quietly and then said, "but sir, it was you who phoned me at the last minute and urgently requested for a van. And when I told you there was none at present, you pleaded that I send any van and I had no choice but to send the van which was in our garage for a complete overhaul!"

3

On Taking Things as They Come

Growing up as a girl was rather difficult two decades back. I had a lot of restrictions at home. When my father was around, he would order me to go and study if he saw me speaking to my relatives. He did not like me talking to the neighbours either. Talking aloud or laughing was also taboo. Hence, I grew up very shy and reserved.

But, I was lucky and never felt bored or even the need to go out and make friends as I enjoyed playing with my siblings – three brothers and a sister. We played together all the time, quarreled, studied and did a lot of amusing things together. Being the eldest, I was very caring and loved my siblings so much that I interfered in everything they did.

My mother was completely different from my father. In her presence, I would feel free as a bird and say whatever was on my mind. I would also talk to people without feeling shy. I particularly adored her because she would send me on errands very often and that gave me a little freedom, to see what the world looked like beyond school and home. But the places she would send me to, were just a street away. It could be the petty shop at the corner of the road to buy provisions or to the maid servant's house to enquire why she had not turned up or to the grinding mill to have the flour ground.

Of all the places my mother sent me, the errand I enjoyed most was going to call the doctor, because it was three streets away and it took considerable time to reach there. He was the only available doctor in town, and whenever my mother fell ill, she would tell me to go and fetch him. I would be so happy that I would skip through all the way, along with my sister or brother.

Getting us five children ready for school, was taxing for my mother. She would get up early in the morning at 4.30 A.M. everyday and work up to 9.30 A.M. and after seeing my father off to office, set about tidying the house. Again she would prepare special lunch for my father, who would come home in the afternoons. She would then have a short nap and we children would disturb her by knocking hard on the door at 3.30 P.M. Then she would get up and start her work all over again. I remember, how she would fold our uniforms and press them by keeping them under the pillows for we did not have an iron then. With this kind of hectic life, she would fall sick very often and I would have the opportunity to run and call the doctor.

The doctor's clinic was a small and narrow room with mud walls and was always dimly lit. There was a small table on which he placed his paraphernalia and a wooden chair on which he usually sat and attended to his patients. A small steel stool was placed near the table for the patients to sit and it rocked badly every time anyone sat on it. At a time, only two persons could feel comfortable inside. Those were the days, when people did not think it necessary to visit a doctor. They believed in nature cure and tried all sorts of remedies at home. So the doctor would very often be seen standing outside with his hands at the back, chatting with the people on the road. It could be a peasant or a shepherd driving his cattle home or it could be a young girl collecting cow dung from the road to use as fuel.

On seeing the doctor, I would inform him that mother was not feeling well and ask him to drop in before going home. He would give a brief nod. He would then promptly come to our house on his bicycle after closing his clinic at 8 P.M. With his black worn-out bag, he would come in and examine my mother. Then, he would give her some large pills and ask her to swallow them two at a time. My mother would pop them into her mouth immediately. In the morning, I would find her busy in the kitchen cooking and carrying on with her usual chores in the midst of the hustle and bustle of sending us all to school.

On some days, when my father was at home, after attending to my mother, the doctor would sit with him and have a chat. The doctor was never in a hurry. He was a man who had all the time in the world for anyone who wished to have a conversation with him.

Once, when I had gone on a similar errand to the clinic, the doors were open, but the doctor was not in. After a thorough search, I found him sitting in the adjoining tailor's shop, learning to fasten a button onto a shirt. From then on, whenever I went to call the doctor, I found him in the tailor's shop, where he would be learning his new trade and one fine day, to my surprise, I found him at the sewing machine stitching a shirt.

During one of his visits to our house, I saw him discussing something very serious with my father. Both of them were talking in hushed tones, and so in spite of lingering around them, I could not even get the gist of it. Nor did I like to stand there and listen to them. However, I learnt about it the next day, from my mother. She told me that Father was getting a loan of Rs.800 from his office to purchase a sewing machine.

Though a Civil Engineer working in a Government organization, my father could never make both ends meet and there was always an acute shortage of money at home. He had always wished to start sort of business to augment his income. He had made many an attempt to do some construction job privately, but my mother was against it and never allowed him and instead, asked him to take care of us and be satisfied with what God had given. When the doctor told him that he had learnt tailoring and that he could stitch blouses for the ladies and augment his income, my father was ready to offer him help by purchasing a sewing machine. He also advised him to carry out his part-time job from our house itself and a memorandum of understanding was reached between them that they would share the earnings equally.

On the day the sewing machine arrived a small crowd had gathered, curious to know what we were up to. My mother explained it all to them. After this, many of our neighbours also started attending tailoring classes regularly. We children were not allowed to touch the sewing machine and hence waited eagerly for the doctor to come, so that we could have a glimpse of the machine, when the doctor worked on it.

The summer vacations were coming to an end and it was time for school to reopen. Every year, on the first day, almost all the students wore new uniforms to school except us. In order to meet his budget my father purchased our school uniforms only on our birthdays or during festive occasions when it was compulsory to wear new clothes. But this year, he bought material for the uniforms for all my brothers and they were very thrilled. Probably, he wished to save money on tailoring expenses as well as keep the doctor busy.

The next day, our doctor arrived at sharp 11 a.m. (Expln. Colloquial made literary) We stopped our games abruptly and surrounded the doctor to watch him operate the new sewing machine and stitch the half pants and shirts for my brothers. He took out the sheet on which he had noted down the measurements and cut the navy blue cloth dexterously. My mother reminded him from the kitchen about father's advice that the uniforms should be made a little loose – for children grow very fast and they should be able to wear it at least for another two years. He laboured over the job, cutting and stitching the uniforms and one fine day it was done and ready. He waited for my father to return from office. On his arrival, he handed over the uniforms which he had sewed (colloquial made literacy) so painstakingly. My father was very anxious that my brothers try them out immediately. He summoned my brothers one by one and asked them to wear them. My first brother, with joy writ large on his face, tried on his new outfit very carefully so as not to soil it, while the rest of us stood at a distance watching the reaction on my father's face. On seeing my brother in his new uniform, it was with great difficulty that we were able to muffle our laughter. The pants were so loose that my brother could have easily inserted both legs through one side of the pant itself. It was the same with my other two brothers' uniforms as well. The doctor knew that he had committed a blunder but he concealed it by telling us that Father had wanted the uniforms to be stitched very loose. However, he assured my father that he could alter them suitably. This he did in great earnest, several times, until the pants acquired a distinctive shape. My brothers were reluctant to wear the Bermuda shorts to school and their trauma was relieved when Father finally told them to use it at home and promised to have another pair tailored with the help of a proper tailor.

But the doctor did not give up. He attended tailoring classes and practiced on our sewing machine everyday. One day, he did not turn up and after a few months, we heard that the doctor had got a job in a garment factory that exported their goods.

The sewing machine remained in our house for quite a few years gathering dust and grime. However much my father tried to convince my mother to learn tailoring, she would not budge, telling him that she had no time for it. One fine day, my father sold the sewing machine to his friend for half the rate and we children were happy about the extra space we gained at home.

When I feel restless and out of step with the world, I always think about this doctor. It gives me extra vigour and confidence in life. Like a chameleon, which changes its colours in order to adapt to its surroundings, the doctor had changed his own lifestyle and profession to meet his requirements. Also, during moments of displeasure, when I find it very difficult to adjust to change, I think about the easy-going nature of the doctor who very casually recast his whole life to fit in with circumstances.

4

On Looking Young

It was another Monday morning with the usual hustle and bustle of getting the children ready for school. I had got up very late that day because of late night and so was not ready on time. I usually accompanied my husband to the railway station, from where we would part and go to our respective offices. However, I was given five minutes to get ready while my husband went out to take the car from the shed.

I was standing in front of the mirror, giving final touches to my make-up, when all of a sudden, I caught a glimpse of a strand of grey hair. This upset me and I stood there, staring into the mirror but then I heard my husband honking, signalling that it was time to leave. Grabbing my bag and, I scurried down the steps two at a time, to avoid my husband nagging me for not being punctual. Swiftly opening the door, I got in and sat beside him quietly. He began grumbling and I was not in the mood for an argument that day, for my mind was preoccupied with something else!

I was disturbed about the strand of grey hair. I felt that I was not paying much attention to my body and if things continued in this manner, it would go beyond my control and I would become a granny very soon, that too when I was hardly in my mid-thirties. I made a mental note of the various measures I would have to adopt in order to restore the "young girl" look, all over again.

One by one, I listed the measures to be taken. In the first place, I was determined to reduce my tummy and waist. That would make me look considerably younger. Though, there were gyms and health clubs close by, I could not find the time to go to one, nor did I like to squander my hard-earned money on lavish pursuits. Dieting and exercise was the best bet and I decided to give it a try.

The next thing of importance was hair care. I resolved to consult my colleague who had dark, lustrous hair, in spite of her age – she was close to fifty. I was sure that a chat with her would prove to be very useful. I planned to meet her during lunch hour and obtain a few tips.

With a slim body and beautiful mane taken care of, all that I now had to bother about was how to get rid of the freckles, black spots and blemishes and have a soft and smooth facial skin. While ruminating on how best to solve the problem, I thought of browsing through the pages of beauty magazines. And, I was bent on starting early from office that day, so that I could find some at the bookstall and pick up a few tips to look better. That would surely do the trick. Well! the agenda had been made for a mega project and all that mattered now was how best it could be implemented.

All the while, my husband was muttering something under his breath while my mind was filled with the targets and goals I had set. When at last, he noticed that I was keeping quiet without showing any reaction to his lecture, he said in exasperation, "I am speaking to you". All that was left was for me was to execute the agenda in the best possible manner. I nodded thoughtfully. *Yes! I am pretty serious about it and I am going to strive to achieve my end.* When my husband saw me nodding my head, he was happy thinking that I had listened to him patiently without arguing. He dropped me off at the station and we went our separate ways. Poor man, if he only knew that I had not heard a word of what he had spoken, he would sue me. But then, it was for him, that I was exerting myself so much, to bring back the "young girl" look – for him to feel proud of his young and beautiful wife and believe that beauty transcends age!

However, the mega project which had begun in great earnest ended in sheer failure! That day, while on my way back to the house, I spent a lot of time at the bookstall scrutinising the various beauty magazines stacked on a number of racks and picked up a few which I thought might be useful to me. Later, I scanned through these magazines and jotted down the tips which met my requirements.

The theoretical parts having been completed, I started to put them into practice. Very soon, my dressing table was filled with all kinds of foundation creams, cold creams and many herbal products. Of course, I had to pay through my nose for them! After using them for just a few weeks, I developed a skin rash and my face and hands kept itching all the time. Then to cure my skin allergy, I had to run from one dermatologist to another.

I wondered what exactly had gone wrong and once again patiently went through the magazines word by word. And there it was! Each of the magazines had clearly specified that one had to test the type of skin whether it was normal, oily or dry and then select the right kind of product that suited the skin type. Well! Trying to find out my skin type and then choosing the right type of product that suited my skin, I realised, would take aeons ! Why, it may even take an entire lifetime, and I gave up the very concept of baby soft skin then and there.

My next objective was to reduce weight by exercise and dieting. After two Caesarian operations, the doctor had advised me not to do any strenuous exercises and the best exercise was walking and so I began walking home from the station everyday which took me about half an hour.

There was an old lunch box, the lid of which had been lost long back. It had been lying in the cupboard gathering dust all the while. All of a sudden, its value appreciated for it was going to help me reduce my weight. I wished to use this as a rationing cup to measure the quantity of rice that I was allowed to consume everyday in order to lose weight.

After a month, I checked my weight and was rather shocked to learn that I had in fact gained a kilo. I was reminded of the day my husband had scoffed at my idea of using this measuring cup. I had stuffed rice into it up to the brim and emptied it into my plate. Looking at the large amount of rice, he had said, "This is more than the quantity you normally consume!" I had been quick to retort then and asked him to mind his own business.

The next day, the tiffin box went back to the cupboard with the same enthusiasm with which it had been brought out. I abandoned the measuring cup and with it the idea of having rice. Subsequently, I started living on fruits and vegetables for a while. As a result, I began to feel weak and developed a haggard and bleary look! Also, this resulted in further loss of hair!

Regarding the hair care tips I had received from my colleague, I just could not implement them for she had advised me to take foods stuff which were inappropriate for a person on a diet and would hamper my efforts to look slim. No wonder, my friend was rather plump! And so, all my attempts at "looking young" had done me as much good as a tissue paper dress in a rainstorm!

Cupping my chin with both my hands, I was sitting all alone, on the portico, deliberating my next move towards attaining my objective, when Madam Sudarshanma's face loomed large in front of my eyes! Memories of her came flooding back.

She was our Social Studies Teacher and was in her mid Thirties. Her hair was completely grey, which she rolled up into a neat bun. A kind and understanding teacher, she was also everyone's favourite. She never uttered a harsh word. This fact endeared her to us and she would begin the class by telling us a story for the first ten minutes before continuing with the lesson. She insisted that all of us call her *Behenji* (sister) and not Miss and if we did, we would only miss her.

There were a few students around her all the time and on days we did not have her class, we sneaked out during the recess period, just to greet her! Even the most shy student would come out of her shell in her presence.

We also took a certain amount of liberty with her. Noticing that she had just two cotton sarees, which she wore on alternate days, we coaxed her to buy some more sarees. She readily heeded our request and wore a new saree the following week, just to please us!

Although she was not very attractive, she wore the most beautiful make-up - her smile! She would flash a smile at each and everyone who came across her, without any discrimination. She earned our undying admiration.

The thought of her bolstered my confidence and a new realisation dawned on me! It is not just the external beauty that is of great importance; the inner beauty - the beauty of the heart mattered much more! One had to know how to get along with others, without hurting them in any way. And so I resolved to change my life and also modify my way of thinking. I would rather not wound anybody's feelings and also see to it that all whom I came across would feel better and happier for having met me!

How graciously had Madam Sudarshanma accepted old age without any regrets! So would I! After all, ageing is a natural process and I was going to accept it joyfully. Each stage of life has its own joys and sorrows and I was determined to experience every moment of it!

Time robs our youth, friends and everything- and all that lives of us, is the love we have given to others! Ever since, I began viewing life with this new perception, I have had had no compunctions about ageing!

5

It Rattles On

As the train approached the station, I jostled my way across, to the exit and breathed a sigh of relief on successfully stepping out of the train, on to the platform. When I looked back, for a moment, I felt foolish, for the train was by far empty and I could have got down without much fuss. On that day, I had actually started early from my workplace, which was much before the peak hour rush and unmindful of the fact, I had hustled my way through, by force of habit !

Everyday, I travel by train to office and the journey back and forth takes about an hour. Compartments are jam-packed and without pushing and shoving one cannot enter or get down from the train. Even travelling first class does not make any difference during the peak hours. Every time a station approaches, there is a lot of shouting and swearing and one can hear all sorts of ridiculous bickerings by even the so-called well-educated people. Seeing them, I would be reminded of the fights the folks generally have at the street corner while queuing up near the corporation taps for water.

People would rebuke one another, calling each other names and would continue with their tirade till the next station, when once again, a fresh crowd would rush in. Very often, the two women who were quarrelling all the while would become friends and embark upon a new quarrel with some other lady treading on their shoes. Being a keen observer, I would get to hear interesting stories and enjoyed watching the facial expressions of the people involved in the quarrel. However I made it a point, never to open my mouth even when I was at fault. Once, I had stepped on someone's foot and the lady had screamed in pain. She started yelling at me, and I pretended to look elsewhere, so that people wouldn't know at whom she was actually shouting.

Everyday, I get to experience funny incidents which leave an indelible impression on my mind. One day, as I entered the train and stood in the midst of a packed crowd, a lady in front of me dragged my handbag along with hers. However much I tugged at my bag, she would not let go of it and I stopped making any further attempts for I was sure that it would be safe inside the train and I had two more stations to go. Once the lady got space to stand and was comfortably settled, she felt something heavy in her hand and wondered how it got there. All the while I stood observing her to see how she would react to the extra baggage. As she looked up, her eyes met mine and I could not help but laugh out loud.

Travelling during peak hours is an opportunity for young men to show-off their skills. Many of them wait for the train to start, and keep running after it for a while and finally climb into the compartment when the train picks up speed. In bygone days, men tried to outdo one another by testing their skills and strength in the use of bow and arrow, or bullfighting or even fighting battles. These days, the trend is to evoke a sense of inspiration and awe in the minds of people by boarding a running train – and greater the speed of the train, greater is the quantum of such feelings they elicit. They imagine themselves as big heroes, in the midst of a film shoot. They are hardly aware of the fact that their own life is at stake.

Quite often, I happened to hear stories of misfortune too. Once a lady stood at the exit with the end of her saree *pallu* flying in the air. It got entangled in an electric pole and she fell of the train. From that day onwards, I became extra careful to tuck in the *pallu* of my saree and not let it fly loose. Thus, on seeing the train approach, I prepare to board it by first tucking in the saree *pallu* firmly and then lifting the saree high up so that people do not trip over it. In this manner, I board the train ready to confront the crowd. It so happens, that while travelling during rush hour, all you have to do is to somehow manage to step into the train and the rest will be taken care of by the surging crowd which pushes you to the other end of the compartment. One day, caught up in reading a book, I was unaware of the approaching train. Hastily, I forced my way in and was at once reminded about the ritual of tucking my saree. So, I collected the *pallu* of my saree, and was attempting to tuck it in but found that something was holding it up and as I pulled it harder, the lady behind me barked, "will you please stop tugging and leave my saree alone!"

One day, there was a signal failure and the trains got unusually delayed. Being very particular about reaching home on time, I took great pains that day to enter into the compartment of the first delayed train. However, getting off the train was very cumbersome. As the station was nearing, I even offered a small prayer to God seeking His help in getting out of the train, for many a time, even with an all-out effort, the ladies miss their stations and are forced to get down only at the next one. That particular day, I was rather lucky and my efforts to get off train met with success. That day proved to be a memorable one for yet another reason. It was the day I happened to stumble upon the false hair that had slipped off a lady's head. The lady was quick to realize that something was wrong and bent down and picked up her wig, which was her precious possession and once again fixed it on her head. She was embarrassed beyond her wits and without looking back, ran up the steps, two at a time.

Things got worse when I became pregnant. Commuting in crowded trains was going to be a real problem and my friends advised me to travel only by first class. Even my husband who was a little tight-fisted when it came to spending cash, told me to I take a first class pass. But I did not agree with him for I felt that it actually made no difference to me and the only difference it would make was that I would be able to stand comfortably without being squashed. Many people joked that I could save expenses by not having to go to a hospital for delivery, as the people on that train would take care of it. This was too much for me and the last straw on the camel's back. I chalked out a plan to tide over the crisis. Undaunted, I started travelling on the footboard. At each station, I would get off the train and board it after everyone stepped in. The women were kind enough to give me some space to stand comfortably. This way, my protruding belly was outside the compartment. Some women warned me about the risk I was taking and offered me a seat or readily moved aside so that I could enter without being squashed. But I refused curtly telling them that my baby was much safer outside the compartment!

One fine day, a man who was frantic to reach office on time, ran to board the train. He entered a compartment and finding all ladies inside, thought he had made a mistake and ran forward to the next compartment and once again there were women inside. He ran further in search of his usual men's compartment but not finding one, sighed heavily. His confusion was set right when an elderly man sitting on the platform cried out, "This is the ladies' special train".

The year 1999 had indeed begun on a happy note for me and for thousands of other women who travelled by train. Some kind soul had at last taken pity on the womenfolk and to lessen the problems faced by them everyday, introduced special trains "for women only" during the peak hours. How my life changed after this! I now made it a point to travel only by the Ladies' Special (LS) train which was almost always empty. There was no need to push and shove and as the train reached the station, I would board it in a relaxed manner, devoid of tension. There was sufficient space for everyone to sit. Everyday, I had a feeling that I was on a picnic or the women made it appear so. A group of people sang devotional songs in a melodious tune and I enjoyed listening to them and got carried away into a spiritual realm. Some plugged in their Walkman, some relished their breakfast, and some did their hair. And, I had an opportunity to listen to the conversations of people around me. It could be a discussion about their tough boss and how she was going to tackle him, or it could be a nice recipe or handy household tip to tide over common problems or tips on beauty and health care. The compartment was like a miniature TV where I got to know the latest talk of the town. The old women, who were still forced to work or were at the verge of retirement, resorted to a short nap stretching out their legs.

But there is always another aspect of a story. The men were unhappy with the introduction of the Ladies' Special as it was a hindrance to them. At the workplace the men who reached office late due to the running of the LS train, cursed the General Manager who had introduced the train and claimed that he was a henpecked husband and had introduced it for his wife to do shopping. Some would sarcastically talk behind our backs, that coffee and tiffin would also be served to the women travelling in the LS train in due course and thus free the ladies from the burden of having their breakfast at home. On the platform, it was even worse. Everywhere, men could be heard passing silly comments on ladies. Once, while I was about to board the LS train, a stout man yelled to his friend, "It is a woman's world these days and who the bloody hell cares for men! It is the ladies who are in the forefront everywhere these days !" Some men rebelled by climbing into the LS train for they could not bear to see it so roomy. Such lawlessness was curtailed very soon, with the introduction of a police escort in each compartment. Also, each day, before the arrival of the LS train, the stationmaster announce or rather reminds the public that the male passengers are requested not to enter in. The police force ensured that not even a single male beggar or vendor boarded the train. Men who got on the train inadvertently were also dealt with severely. One day, a man was walking on the platform, close to the LS train, when out of the blue a harsh voice was heard, "keep away from the train, it is the LS train ! You could be booked for trespassing !" The man who was probably daydreaming, was startled on hearing the rasping tone, and bolted from there instantly.

Once, a lady who was in her final stage of pregnancy came into our compartment. She was going to the hospital for a check-up and finding two seats empty, she comfortably reclined on it and closed her eyes. Her husband who was not allowed to accompany her, was to meet her by the next train. All of a sudden, she got her labour pains and began to panic. She met the police escort in the compartment who came to her rescue. At the next station, the policewoman met the stationmaster and an announcement was made requesting help. Fortunately, a lady doctor was travelling in that train and she was ready to help her out and the lady was blessed with a boy. The train halted for some time and many of us ran to take a peek at the "train child".

The hue and cry to cancel the LS train only fell on deaf ears and the top brass stuck to their guns! With the passage of time the snide comments reduced and nowadays we don't get to hear many complaints. Probably, people have adapted themselves to the change! The LS train goes past everyday, bringing cheer to women and catering to their needs. Though the tongues continue to wag once in a while, the Ladies' Special train rattles on. For how long, no one can say !

6

The Wanderers

My mother often told me that as a child I was so unruly that she had to found different ways to tackle my tantrums and misdemeanour. She often scared me with stories about gypsies, who were coming to take me away. During meals when I refused to eat anything, she would threaten me that the gypsies were on their way and I would immediately eat everything on my plate.

Similarly, when I refused to sleep, she would pretend to call up the gypsies and I would then shut my eyes tightly and fall asleep instantly. In this way, my mother had nurtured a sort of fear in my mind regarding these gypsies.

Every time the gypsies passed by our street, the dogs chased them, barking furiously. On hearing the ferocious barking of the dogs, I would flee the place, screaming, for I believed that the gypsies were in the vicinity. Once, I asked Mother, why the dogs always pursued the gypsies and she told me a convincing fairy tale. Years back, when the world began, the dog was selected by man as his best and faithful friend. Once, the head of the gypsy tribe promised to give his daughter in marriage to his trustworthy dog but never kept his word. Since then, whenever the gypsies are around, the dogs bark their heads off.

When I was just five years old and studying in the first standard, my father hired an old man to pick me up after school. One fine day, when I stepped out of the class, I was dismayed to see that the servant had not turned up. I waited for one long hour with the hope that he would come to take me home but he never turned up. The sun was beginning to set and so I decided to walk home. I was familiar with the long route back home which was about twelve Km, but I was scared of the gypsies who roamed the streets with guns. However, having no other choice as the school grounds were almost empty and the teachers had also left, I started walking slowly. I had to traverse busy roads which I carefully crossed.

A lonely stretch of red sand road began which was where the gypsies were seen often, hunting birds and other small animals. Fear gripped me as I continued to walk. Then in the distance I saw them – a gang of gypsies walking towards me. They were skimply dressed in dirty, torn clothes. The men carried big guns with them. I was very frightened and I immediately started running, with tears rolling down my cheeks. But the gypsies did not even notice me and walked by, chatting in a peculiar language which I could not understand. How thrilled I was then! I understood that the gypsies were not dangerous after all and wouldn't try to shoot me. Their guns were used for shooting birds and animals, to eke out their living and they certainly did not kill humans.

That day, I felt I had conquered the world and was eager to recount my adventure to my mother. When I reached home, I saw her waiting outside, with a worried look on her face. She must have been wondering, why I had not yet returned from school. With great excitement, I began to narrate the story of encountering the gypsies. After listening patiently, she marvelled at my courage in crossing the busy roads and the gypsies.

After this incident I was never afraid of gypsies. From then on, whenever I heard the dogs barking frantically, I would run out to see if the gypsies were there. I would stare at their clothes and admire the colourful bead chains and thick bangles adorning their necks and hands and marvel at the sight of tiny babies carried in a sling tied round their mother's necks.

Many a time, the gypsy men would sell their game – birds and animals which they had shot – and people would gather around them haggling over the price. Sometimes, they would sell pure honey which was also in great demand. I had nothing to do with them; but when the women gypsies passed by our street, I would dance with excitement. They would go around selling, colourful bead chains, needles, pins, clips and toys. I would look longingly at all these things, wanting to possess them all.

Once in a while, the women gypsies would stand in front of our house begging for some food and would not budge until my mother gave them something to eat. Once, a pair of gypsy women stood in front of our gate requesting for food. My mother told them that she had nothing to offer and asked them to leave the place. But the women didn't stir from there and after a while they squatted on the ground, displaying their worthy paraphernalia and pestered her to buy some of the bead chains. One of them told us that with the money she earned she would buy something for the child she carried in the sling.

Feeling sorry for the scrawny child and also being very attracted to the colourful bead chains, I pestered my mother to buy me one and at last she relented. I selected a bright and showy bead chain and Mother agreed to buy me that. She bargained with the gypsy to sell it for half the price but the women did not agree and went away. Later, they returned and sold it at the price my mother had requested.

The next day, I wore the colourful bead chain to school and all my friends praised my choice and admired it and enquired from where I had purchased this wonderful chain. Happily, I divulged to them the source from where I had obtained it. They looked at each other in great astonishment though a crime had been committed and started laughing. It was an embarrassing moment for me and I stopped wearing it to school. After that, I never asked my mother to buy anything from the gypsies.

The gypsies are generally looked down upon by society because they are always unkempt and smelly and most of the time, shabbily dressed.Though civilisation has brought about many changes, these gypsies opted to remain like their ancestors and have not endeavoured to change themselves. They still continue to walk miles together, always in groups, to reach their destination, unmindful of the distances to be traversed. The sun, rain or wind hinders them in no way! They always live for the present and don't think about the future. They are satisfied with the meagre income they earn and manage to eke out a living.

However, though I don't express my innermost feelings, to anyone, I secretly hold on to the memory of these gypsies, and cherish them. I have a great fascination for the simple and carefree life that they lead and at times I envy them. When It comes to lessons on simplicity and a contented life, the gypsies are unmatched. It is we who have to learn these lessons the hard way.

Today, we live in a cyber age with vast advancements in every walk of life. There is cut-throat competition in all fields of activity. There is also a continuous rat race to be the winner, to reach the top of the social ladder, and sometimes, to even be at the top of the world.

No doubt, we all yearn for a comfortable and luxurious life and strive to acquire more and more materialistic things. The various modern gadgets does things for us in a jiffy and so we want to possess all of them. This of course leaves very little room for exercise, and so we keep bloating up day by day. Also, we keep breaking our heads on how best the things possessed by us could be safeguarded from the hands of thieves. We are constantly gripped with a sense of fear and also lose our sleep trying to protect our fortune.

Once our materialistic wants are fulfilled, we don't rest there. Greed pushes us further and we want to accumulate more and more wealth for the future. We are mad to try and excel in every one of our ventures and by exerting ourselves so much, we do quite a lot of damage to both our mind and body. When we lose our tranquility of mind and our health deteriorates, it is only then that we realize that health is better than wealth!

And then, we start running from one doctor to another to recover our health. We are subsequently advised by these doctors to try and reduce our tensions and also do a lot of exercise. Thus begins our quest for the best gymnasiums, health clubs and yoga clubs for keeping our body fit and to the sanatoriums and ashrams, far away from the maddening crowd, for a serene mind.

In fact, it is our mind which is always unsettled and keeps wandering from one goal to another, throughout our lives. Be it admission to the school or college, a job, marriage, a house, or whatever, we are always in pursuit of the best. Our mind always keeps wandering in want of one thing or the other throughout our lifetime. It never rests in peace and we never

experience tranquility of mind nor contentment. Sometimes I wonder if it is not we who are the real wanderers!

7

The Value of Money

My six-year-old daughter returned from school with a prize that she had won in a drawing competition. It was a beautiful mini postbox with a slit, to drop coins into. I congratulated her and advised her to collect coins everyday so that she could buy something with the money she saved. After admiring the prize for quite sometime, she placed it in the showcase, telling me that there was no need for her to save money as we bought her everything that she wanted. For a moment, I did not know whether to be pleased by what she had said, or whether I had deprived her of knowing the feelings of what it is to be in need of something!

I recollected the days when I was young. To inculcate the habit of saving, my father purchased dolls with slits and gave one to each of us and told us to drop a few coins into it everyday. We often vied with each other, to take coins from our parents and drop them into our piggy-doll banks and we kept rattling them now and then to see who had saved more money. However, one fine day, all our collections would be taken out to meet some exigency and the one who had collected the maximum amount would be lauded by father.

My father loved us very much and often boasted that he was the poor father of rich children. He made all efforts to give us a happy and comfortable life. On reaching middle age, he developed arthritis and so every night, requested one of us to massage his aching feet. Though we hated this ritual, out of concern, we took turns in pressing his feet everyday. However, my eldest brother would refuse to massage his feet, unless he wanted something from father. Being the first born son in the family, he got his own way. Once, when father retired for a short siesta on a Saturday afternoon, my brother sat beside him and started massaging his feet. Slowly, he started cajoling him to take us all our for a movie and my father agreed. Later he realised that he had no money with him that day. However he did not wish to disappoint us and so tore off a slip of paper and scribbled a note, requesting the shop owner, from whom we purchased provisions, to send rupees twenty through the bearer of the letter. As my brother ran out, we eagerly waited his return. At last, he appeared before us with a gloomy face and said that the shop owner had refused to help. We were crestfallen and Father promised to take us for a movie, after receiving his salary. Then, with a whoop of glee, my brother suddenly leaped up like a hero, displaying with pride a twenty-rupee note and our joy knew no bounds!

Father was always in desperate need of money to meet one expense or the other. This was also often the subject of controversy between my parents. The words "no money for that" cropped up in each and every conversation they had. Sometimes, it would begin as a small disagreement and end up with a ferocious argument and they would stop talking to each other for almost a week. I would then intercede and get things straightened out. Their frequent bickering, ingrained in me a strong feeling that money is the most important thing in the world and without it, no one respected you. I was determined to work and make a lot of money!

My father presented me a diary on New Year's Eve of 1985. This was a different kind of diary and was titled *The Ideal Home Diary*. It contained small tips on every subject and I treasured it as a reference book. As I scanned the pages, I was rather thrilled to read the information on manufacturing detergent powder and herbal shampoo. After reading it, an idea struck me. This was indeed a very good opportunity to make money! Immediately, I envisioned myself as a busy businesswoman, who made it to the top, by dint of hard labour. I spent the whole day, taking down notes from the book and chalked out a plan for carrying out the project. That night while going to sleep, I experienced a unique satisfaction of having accomplished a great task, and it is not for nothing that it is said "well planned is half done". The list of chemicals that are to be procured was now ready. The next day, I pleaded with mother to buy me some chemical powders from the market, through our shop owner's assistant, a young boy. I had also asked her to get me some wood ash from our neighbour, who still used wood as fuel to cook. It almost took a whole week to gather all the resources to begin my business. *Selling my products will be no problem, as the shop owner will readily agree to sell them,* I reassured myself.

I selected a secluded spot where I would not be disturbed. In front of me were half- kilo packets of various chemicals and a huge quantity of wood ash. Using a measuring cup, I mixed the chemicals in the right proportion and began to spread them over a thick sheet of paper in front of me, in order to remove any lumps and also to get a fine mixture of the detergent powder. It was only an hour after commencing my job, when all of a sudden, I felt a sharp pain in my shoulder joints which was probably due to continuous movements involved in the effort. In a short while, my hips and back also began to ache. *But this can't be an excuse for quitting the work. Hard work alone yields best results. When the business expands, I can always employ a few women, and that is not a big deal,* I told myself. By afternoon, the detergent powder was almost ready. After dusting off the thin layer of chemical coating from my dress, I stretched my hands and legs to relieve the pain.

After having a quick bite, I started making the herbal shampoo. This was much easier and all I had to do was mix the wood ash in water and heat it for a while. After cooling it, I added the necessary chemicals and the shampoo was ready to be stored overnight, after which it could be used. It was dusk when I was done with my job. That night I writhed in acute pain. However, I did not complain, for fear that my parents would advise me to abandon the project. I closed my eyes, yearning for daybreak.

It was an unforgettable day indeed. I woke up very late and my folks had already left. It was 10 a.m., and the maidservant came in. I handed the detergent powder to her, and told her to wash the clothes with it. When she dried out the clothes, I found that the grease marks and the grime were still present.I learnt that the powder did not foam well and hence the stains were reluctant to leave the clothes. Surely, no customer was going to like it ! But I did not regret relinquishing this project, for the body ache I suffered the whole night, alerted me to the fact that, this was not the kind of job that I could handle independently.

But I still had a chance of success.I lifted the bottle of shampoo and observed a thick layer of wood ash sediment at the bottom. I decanted the clear liquid into another bottle and stored it in a corner of the bathroom. I wished to wash my hair with it the next day to test its quality.It was just then, that my little brother returned from school. On seeing him, I changed my mind. Of all the siblings, he was my favourite and eight years younger to me. I adored him, mainly because he would obey me with implicit faith. I explained to him- my first customer

-with great enthusiasm, all about the shampoo, and he was impressed with it. He also agreed to use it immediately. I called him into the bathroom and sat him on the floor. Since it was a home-made herbal shampoo, I was quite liberal and took a handful of it and began applying it on his head. On seeing the handful of shampoo, my brother expressed his fear that it could burn his eyes and I reassured him that it was a herbal one and was those harmless. Unfortunately, the shampoo did not form any lather either. So, I poured out some more and started scrubbing his hair exerting extra pressure. But it was not of much use and there was not enough lather. By now I was under stress by the utter failure of my project and lifting up the bottle, I emptied it fully over his head, hoping that this huge quantity would work up some foam. Sensing that my attempts were in vain, I tried to calm myself. Slowly, I rinsed out his hair with water and with it the idea of becoming a big business woman!

I now turned to God to help me get a job. I offered prayers, both in the morning and evening. Everyday I would stand in front of Him with pleading eyes for quite a few minutes and leave with a satisfaction that He had heard my prayers. At times, when no one was around, would also weep, telling Him to bless me with the best job in the world. Then one day, when I was almost twenty five years old, my prayers were anwered – I got a job. Of course, I had had to wait patiently for such a long time. It was a job of my choice and I enjoyed it tremendously. Everything after that totally changed in my life! There was a constant flow of money. Money gave me everything that I yearned for - a loving husband and pretty children, a large and beautiful mansion and wonderful luxuries of the modern world.

I consider myself lucky, for being showered by God, with the gift of contentment. I was not possessed with the desire to hoard wealth and property; nor was I after fame! Then arrived a particular phase in my life, when there was nothing I was really in need of. I found life boring without any excitement. I loved the stress and strain I experienced all through my life, when I was intent on achieving one goal or the other. All of a sudden, I felt that I was devoid of this need!

Alone at home, one Saturday morning, I was just ruminating over this aspect, when all of a sudden, my thoughts were disturbed by the telephone bell. It was my sister and while chatting with her, I enquired about her little daughter. She started grumbling that her daughter was incorrigible and spent the whole time watching TV in her neighbour's house. As I placed the receiver on the cradie, I remembered that my sister did not have a television at home and that is why her daughter was always away from home!

The next time I visited my sister, I presented a new colour TV to my niece. The little girl was very happy and ran about telling all and sundry in the street that her aunt had bought a TV for her. I too shared in her excitement that day! On seeing the joy writ large on her face, a realization dawned on me - there is indeed an unmatched pleasure in doing something for others, without expecting anything in return !

That day, I learnt a simple truth! Money spent on charity, without expecting anything in return gives us immense joy. It also enhances the value of money many times over.Making others cheerful by helping them in any possible manner gives one fulfilment and happiness. From then on, I made it a point to do some charity work or offer timely succour once in a while and enjoy my efforts to spread happiness !

8

Woman's Day

One Friday evening, as soon as I stepped into the house, my daughter grabbed the bag from my hand and started to examine its contents. After scouring through it fully, she became dejected on not finding her favourite milk sweet, which I had promised her that day. I apologized for forgetting, and instead conceded to make a sweet at home. The next day being a holiday I wished to spare some time for my daughter in preparing Mysore pak, a sweet, which is nothing but a mixture of gram flour, ghee and sugar in the right proportions. I selected this sweet because, of all the sweets, this was the most simple to prepare. However, one had to be pretty careful about details such as the correct consistency, when it should be taken off from the fire and poured out into greased plates for cutting into diamond shapes. Moreover, it was Woman's Day and I thought that my young lady must be honoured suitably with a treat.

After ordering my daughter to carry on with her homework, I entered the kitchen to start preparations for it. While I was halfway through, my daughter, sniffing the aroma of ghee and gram flour that wafted across to her room, came trotting into the kitchen. The mixture in the pan started frothing and I knew for sure that this was the right consistency. Using a pair of tongs, I lifted the pan off the stove and poured the contents on to a greased plate. I let it cool under the fan.

My daughter's taste buds were kindled and she licked her lips in anticipation. She watched me avidly, as I took a sharp knife and slid it through the thick batter. Her mouth began to water and she got ready to have the first bite. When I tried to pull out the knife to make another cut, it refused to budge. My daughter was quick to comment, "perhaps, the knife relishes the sweet too !" Applying my full strength, I succeeded in yanking out the knife from the hardened mixture. I attempted another cut, but this time, the knife did not even pass through it. Something had gone wrong somewhere and I understood that this was not going to taste like the usual Mysore pak - the one which melts in our mouths the moment we take a bite of it. Suddenly an idea flashed through my mind and I left the room in search of a small hammer. My daughter stood there silently, wondering what I was up to!

While scanning the cupboard for a hammer, I was reminded about my mother who, many a times, would give me the waste newspapers and old magazines, to dispose of in the nearby shop. I would get a commission out of selling the scrap papers. With the money earned, I would buy my favourite chocolate called "Kamarakat". It was in the shape of round marbles and was dark brown in colour. The chocolate was rock hard and I would hold it in my mouth for a considerable time, sucking its sweet juice. After some time, I would be able to crack it and then I would try my level best to chew it exerting considerable pressure and finally swallow it.

Nowadays, such chocolates are hard to find and I wished to introduce my daughter to the pleasure of crunching Kamarakat. My daughter continued to stand in the kitchen bemused at the goings-on. I deftly concealed the fact that the

Mysore pak had not turned out well and started breaking the hardened batter into tiny pieces. I offered one piece to her. She popped it into her mouth and grimaced. I advised her that Kamarakat could not be bitten into immediately and explained to her the art of savouring this peculiar sweet.

Generally, while doing her homework, my daughter would come out of her study several times to get doubts cleared. Today she appeared to be in a serious mood and worked out her maths homework all by herself. Probably, she thought that if she came to see me I would pop another piece into her mouth. And she also did not wish to hurt her mother, who had slogged all the while in the kitchen making a sweet, just for her!

The vessels were scattered all around and the kitchen counter was in total shambles. I had a tough time cleaning up the mess. A thick layer of the hardened batter stuck to the bottom of the pan and I was scrubbing it with all my strength, when I heard the doorbell ring. My husband entered and on inhaling the sweet aroma that still lingered in the air asked if I had made any sweet. I told him that since it was Woman's Day I wanted to please my little lady and so had made Kamarakat. On hearing the name, he stood still halfway and said, "who on earth gave you this idea ?" There was no way but to let the cat out of the bag and I explained the whole story, justifying my act. After much coaxing, he picked up a piece and popped it into his mouth.

He used all his might and crushed the sweet into tiny pieces and swallowed it immediately. Suddenly, he felt a sharp pain in his tooth. Just a month back, he had been to a dentist and got a root canal therapy done to cure a tooth-ache. Inadvertently, now he used the very same tooth to bite into the sweet and the pain returned. This infuriated him and he started yelling at me for wasting my time and energy. He shouted that, had I spent the time with my daughter, she would have been much happier. Instead I had wasted both time and provisions in preparing an inedible sweet.

Every month, while buying provisions, my husband and I would have a tiff regarding the things we ought to buy. He would often tell me to be more economical, and advise me to cut down on the expenditure on provisions. However, the moment he commented about my wasting money on provisions, it would get on my nerves and trigger off a fierce argument.

One day, I sat with him and explained patiently that both of us worked just so that we could lead a life of luxury and be able to spend money lavishly. And it was silly of him to keep rebuking me quite often to cut down on the expenditure on provisions. I also warned him that in future if he ever commented about my spending too much on provisions, I would stop eating food at home. He was quick to answer that this would help him save the money. Later, I asked him to promise me that he would never reproach me again over this issue. He agreed and since then had dared not reprove me. Now when the severe toothache returned, he forgot all his resolutions and shouted his head off. I was upset on hearing his harsh words.

I stomped out of the room in disgust. I told him that if he felt I was wasting the provisions, he could very well take care of the cooking and try bringing down the expenditure substantially, and that I would not stand in his way. He then retorted that kitchen work was not destined for men and it was a woman's job!

My daughter who had just finished her studies came out of her room. One seeing her, I realised that it was dinner time already and our bickering stopped abruptly. I started kneading the dough to make rotis all the while ruminating on why the hell were we celebrating Woman's Day!

Is it to create an awareness in society that, unlike bygone days, women have become much stronger ? That we have dared to enter each and every front where men have set foot. That we have climbed the highest mountains, gone into spac and also crossed the biggest oceans. And hence, we are equal to men!

Or is it to warn society that women ought to be treated with dignity, love and kindness. And that any ill-treatment meted out to us, shall be taken care of - for we shall collectively go to any extent in fighting for our rights!

Either way, celebrating Woman's Day will serve little or no purpose. For if the former is true, then we better stop bragging about it! By proclaiming aloud every year that we are strong and equal to men, we are indirectly evincing the fact that we are still considered weak!

On the other hand, in the latter case, fighting for our rights by just celebrating Woman's Day will not be adequate. It is not going to change the perception held by society for so long. For, this very notion that "women are the weaker sex" was handed down to us by the cavemen and for society to change its way of thinking, a vast change has to be brought about in the minds of the people.

When God created the universe, it was the woman's lot to be born with a weak physical condition. The cramps experienced by women during menstruation make her unfit for a few days every month. The pregnancy period is also one of turmoil and the pangs of labour at the time of childbirth need no mention at all! This is then followed by menopausal blues. That's why, the cavemen were naturally protective towards women and let her just take care of the house and children, while they went out to hunt for food!

This caveman thinking has been handed over to us down the ages and for this view to change completely, it will take aeons! Unless society frees itself from the shackles of outdated ways of thinking and understands that cooking for the family, taking care of the children and household work is as much a man's job as it is a woman's, all talk about women's rights, liberation or equality is a sheer waste!

9

A Lesson Learnt

It was almost afternoon, when I returned after a shopping spree. I was too tired to do any work and so I stretched out on the bed to have a siesta. My three-year-old daughter sitting beside me was deeply absorbed in her new toy. However, sleep did not come to me that easily because of the commotion outside.

Out on the portico the crows were cawing frenziedly. They were attempting to build a nest, picking up all the little things from the ground that would be useful to them. I tried my best to chase them off. My daughter too, joined me in the effort. But the moment we went in, they were back at their job, cawing endlessly, gathering things to make their nest. They were tugging out sticks from the broom, nibbling at the coconut fibres and other twigs lying on the ground. Finally, I gave up and let them be.After an hour, the raucous din subsided and I closed my eyes. In a jiffy, I was fast asleep.

One fine morning, as I opened the doors to greet the early dawn, I was amazed to see a lovely nest on the top branch of our neem tree, at the rear side of the house. Two small chicks popped out their tiny black heads from the nest and their parents sat close by, guarding them.

At last, the crows had succeeded in building this wonderful nest that had kept them busy for so long! Now that they were done with the job, we were happy to be relieved from the sound of their persistent cawing. But we had guessed wrong, for the worst was yet to come! The crows were highly protective of their chicks, so much so that we could not even move around at will, for any one who wandered towards the rear side of the house received a sharp peck from them.The cunning crows even dared to enter the house when no elders were in the vicinity and even snatch biscuits from my daughter's hand.I made it a point to go out with protective gear to be safe from these wild crows.

However, our servant girl did not fear the crows. She bravely carried out her chores under the neem tree. The crows too, did not harm her in any way. She had a very dark complexion and so we teased her that the crows identified her with their tribe and she would laugh aloud.

My daughter had a jolly time watching the chicks grow. As soon as she woke up in the morning, she would stand by the window and watch the chicks. She would give us a live commentary on all that the baby crows were doing. Sometimes, during the day, she would watch the crows feeding their chicks, and she would come running, asking me to feed her. The feeding task was simplified considerably due to the chicks. Watching them, she would gobble down all the food I offered her, without any fuss and that saved plenty of time, as I didn't have to run around imploring her to eat. The feeding ritual, which was generally a big ordeal for me, was eased with the advent of the crows.

Sometimes my daughter would plead with me to fill a bowl with breadcrumbs and other eatables and then she would throw a piece or two of these titbits high up in the air. The crows would skilfully swoop down to catch them with their beaks. She enjoyed this game every morning.

The days passed and the chicks grew bigger and started coming out of their nest. One day, my daughter entreated me to accompany her to the open staircase, from where we could have a clear view of the fledglings. I curtly refused, telling her that their parents would attack us and it was not wise to go up now. She left the place quietly and I was pleased that for once she had obeyed. But a little later she returned and continued her pleading that the chicks' parents were not around and had gone to get food for their babies. She was not willing to give up and I had to relent for fear that she would start another tantrum of hers and I would have to endure another long verbal battle with her.

We climbed up the stairs very cautiously, watching if the parent crows were around. I also had a stick in my hand which I kept rotating over my head like a fan for protection. Then, all of a sudden, a crow swooped down from nowhere and I felt a sharp jab on my head. Screaming in pain and anger, I slapped my daughter. She ran down the steps crying.

On hearing the commotion, her grandmother came out and took her away, wiping her tears and comforting her. She asked her why she was crying. I knew my daughter was going to blame me for smacking her hard and waited patiently for her to finish off with her story, before I could justify my act. But what I heard from her had me transfixed !

Slowly, she narrated the whole story of dragging me upstairs, to view the baby crows and how in spite of all precautions, the crows had attacked me. She then told her granny that she had cried not because I had whacked her, but because she could not bear to see me in pain. And she lamented that it was due to her that the crow had pecked me. On hearing these words, my heart melted and I regretted my harsh behaviour. Hugging and caressing her, I apologised for spanking her.

I was filled with happiness throughout the day for being blessed with a loving daughter, who was so concerned about the pain I was suffering quite unmindful of the fact that I had hit her.

It was twilight and time for our usual coffee. I was standing in front of the stove, waiting for the milk to boil. The sun had already set and as darkness swept across I was engulfed with a sudden fear.

Hundreds of questions crossed my mind in quick succession. Would my daughter nurture the same kind of love once she grew into a young lady? If she would be influenced by her peers. Would she then heed my advice if I felt she was being misguided ? Would she listen to what her old mother said - for whom she wept so much - whose pain she could not endure?

When she was busy, trying to accomplish the goals of her life, would she have time for her old mother then? Would she sit by my side and talk about how she spent her day and seek my advice and guidance which I would be yearning to offer her. For then, I would be retired and have all the time in life and would be only too willing to share the experiences of my life with anyone who wished to listen patiently. I became rather worried about losing my daughter's love. Luckily, by then, the milk came to a boil and I snapped out of the dreadful mood.

The next day, we left on a pilgrimage for a week. Everyday, my daughter asked me several questions regarding the development of the chicks. How big would they have grown? Could they fly on their own? Did their mother still feed them? I cleared all her doubts one after another. On the last day, she was happy to return home and see her friends.

On reaching home, we ran to the neem tree to look for the birds. We were rather shocked by what we saw! The place wore a very desolate look and the chicks were gone. There was no trace of the crows either. The nest lay in total shambles. The neem tree which had earlier buzzed with hectic activity, was still and silent!

My daughter hounded me with myriad questions. With great difficulty, I explained to her that since the chicks had grown big enough, they had flown off to fend for themselves and did not require their parents' help. But she was not convinced. However, on that day, I learnt a valuable lesson in life!

My mind dwelt on the crows! They had taken so much trouble, building a superb nest to shelter their chicks. And when the chicks were old enough to take care of themselves, how easily, they had let them go - without any regrets! They had all the while provided the chicks with warmth, food and shelter, as long as they needed it and once they were capable of fending for themselves, let them venture into fresh pastures and stopped their interference!

That night while offering my prayers, I begged God to give me the strength to let go off things easily and not be possessive in nature! To help me not be selfish and expect my daughter to return the love and care that I had bestowed upon her, which was after all my duty for bringing her into this world! Like the dutiful crows, all I had to do was build a nest for her - a safety net- and to see to it that she got shelter and warmth from the winds and storms of life! And once her wings were stronger, to let her fly her own way in search of fresh pastures in life!

10

The Eucalyptus Leaves

The cuckoo was cooing frantically and its mate who was far off was answering the call in a similar tone. I stood near the window, gazing at the birds, listening to their melodious tunes. A cool and wet breeze was blowing across, heralding the coming of monsoons. The lush greenery all around soothed my rather turbulent mind. At once, the drabness which had prevailed during the early hours of the day, disappeared and I too felt energetic. I yearned to spend the rest of the day in a worthwhile manner!

Deliberating on how best to spend the day, I swiftly turned back, when the large rack with glass doors caught my eye. The books in it had been untouched for a very long time and they were covered with a thick layer of dust. I decided to dust the books and stack them all over again.These were the books I had read during my school days and with great difficulty had carried them to my new home after marriage.

Carefully, I dusted each book and arranged them in a proper order. I was filled with satisfaction for having accomplished a great task and as I forced the voluminous novel of Leo Tolstoy's The Resurrection into the small gap available, a few eucalyptus leaves fell out of the book. The green colour of the leaves had faded and the fragrance had also gone. However, the memories associated with these leaves was still fresh! I was suddenly overcome with nostalgia and the past came flooding into my mind ....

It was the year 1985 and I had just completed school. Rains lashed the city non-stop for almost a week. Very soon, Madras (now Chennai) was flooded. There were many huts in the low-lying areas surrounding our house, built of clay with thatched roofs. These huts were submerged in water and the people living there were scurrying across the road looking for safer places. Men and women carrying all their important paraphernalia, some of them also carrying their small children on their shoulders, who were shivering in the damp cold moved down the road looking for shelter. I felt very sorry for them!

Slowly, the level of water kept rising. Luckily we were safe because our house was situated on a higher area. All around there was water and some of the cows, buffaloes and stray dogs had drowned. There was no electricity anywhere and the only source of information regarding the weather was the transistor, which kept blaring in our neighbour's house, warning people about further rains and also advising them to move to places at a higher level.

I was undaunted by the floods until one dark evening, when I saw water near our gate. As time passed, the water seeped through the gate and reached the entrance of our house. I saw our neighbours locking their doors and leaving their homes to seek refuge in a hostel nearby. They advised us to join them but we refused with the plea that the rains would stop very soon.

We had probably guessed wrong! It was midnight and my sister woke up saying that her dress was fully wet. My mother lit a lamp and was shocked to find that the water was gradually seeping into our house too. My sister and I tried our best to remove the water with a mop but it proved futile. Later we used a mug to dish out the water and finally gave up, as the water kept gushing in continuously.

My brothers then began lifting the things from the floor and put them in the loft. All of a sudden, we heard a loud bang and ran out to see what had happened. The house opposite our's had collapsed and luckily there were no casualties, for all the people had already left the place. Immediately we were struck with fear and we started discussing our course of action. My father then suggested that early next morning we too should move out and take refuge elsewhere! However, he stated that he wished to stay behind to take care of the things and promised to join us in case the floods turned worse.

Though it was early morning, it was still dark. All around people were carefully walking in the hip-deep water.We too joined the trek! Far off, a dog was yelping aloud and this bad omen filled me with panic and I wondered whether we would return home safely or get lost in the melee. As, I gingerly waded through the cold water my teeth chattered and sharp cold winds cut across my face !

Frightening images flashed across my mind. There was a large manhole in the middle of the road. I continue walking slowly and suddenly I fall into it and sink unnoticed by anybody. I brushed aside these alarming thoughts and continued wading through the water, my toes now strongly gripping the soil but the images kept flashing. The level of water keeps mounting. The water rises to my neck, then slowly to my nose and then covers my eyes. I struggle for breath and is suddenly swept off my feet and the gushing water carries me away. I cry out for help - a cry that is not heard by anyone!

Just then, an old man with a wrinkled face joined me and immediately I broke loose from the wild fantasies! He was holding a stick for support. Seeing my terror-stricken face, he said nonchalantly, "Be courageous young girl! Don't get cowed down by such trifles. There is still a lot more in life and you must learn to face the hardships of life bravely; the rest is His Will - for nothing happens except by His Will!" I looked at the old man's face and tried to force a smile. There was not a trace of fear or anxiety on his face! Probably he was one of those who had got used to the adversities of life!

On reaching the hostel we found that it was already crammed with people. That night I did not sleep and prayed to God to help us out. Many others did the same thing and at last, in response to our fervent prayers, the rains stopped. Early in the morning, the sky cleared up and the sun shone brightly.

I was happy to see a flock of white cranes flying in the sky, in search of food. The sight of the sun delighted everyone. I felt that I was seeing the sun after ages. The crows who had been sitting huddled on the top branches, flew off cawing excitedly. The dogs came out from hiding, wagging their tails, welcoming the sun and the birds in the trees around chirped madly. The insects too wriggled out of the soggy soil!

Small children started making paper boats and floated them in the puddles of water. All around, people seemed to revel in the warmth of the sun. We noticed that the level of water was slowly receding and many people started making a move towards home. We too began our journey back home!

Our journey back home was quite a pleasure!The broad roads were flanked by trees on both sides and water was dripping from the leaves. As we strolled by, I kept rustling the leaves within my reach and enjoyed the feel of the cool water trickling down my face. We reached a particular spot where the damp earth was fully covered with eucalyptus leaves that had been swept away by the furious winds and its fragrance wafted in the air. It seemed as though we were walking on a soft green carpet. Bending down, I picked up a few leaves and inhaled its strong scent.

Throughout the way, I kept smelling the leaves. Even after reaching home, I could not part with them. I was then reading Tolstoy's novel The Resurrection and I insertd these leaves into the thick book, using them as a bookmark.

Putting the eucalyptus leaves back into the book, I chuckled at the silly fears that had gripped me then! But these are the little fears that we grow up with, which in the long run, strengthen our mind and make us confident in life! It enables us to face the severe blows that life sometimes deals us time and again ; like the old man with the wrinkled face!

11

The Child In Us

There was perfect silence in the classroom and all of us were deeply absorbed in a lecture. The topic of the lecture was reproduction. The biology teacher was happy to note that for once , he had captured the attention of each and every student in the class. Quite often, we students took advantage of his lenient nature, and there would be a constant murmur during his class as we whispered amongst ourselves. He would ignore our gossiping and continue his lecture in a full-throated voice.

But on this particular day, there was absolute silence and all of us were deeply engrossed in his lecture. Probably it could be because of the interesting nature of the topic. The teacher was inspired by our silence and got even more animated. He continued talking with great vigour and enthusiasm.

All of a sudden, a stout and tall boy sitting in the first row, started clapping his hands vigorously. The master was astonished and he stopped his lecture, while the rest of the class burst into laughter. He then approached the student and asked him why he had clapped his hands. When the boy did not answer, our teacher yelled at him, "do you think you are watching a comic film or do I look like a circus clown?" The student only hung his head in shame for he did not have any convincing explanation to offer.

This incident happened in the eleventh standard. Many a time, I thought about the chap who behaved in such a queer manner. I would then try and figure out the various reasons that could have prompted him to act in such a crazy manner.

He may have been reminded of a funny joke which could not be revealed openly. Or else, he was perhaps harbouring a dirty secret in his mind not fit to be aired in public. Or it could just be that he had given in to his childish urge to see what would be the consequence of clapping in the midst of a silent class, absorbed in the lecture and to see the reaction of the very lenient teacher.

Sometimes, in life, we come across situations when our emotions and feelings cease to be under our control. The mind becomes our boss and dictates terms to us. That happens when the child in us takes over and we are forced to give in. Under such an impulse, we fail to consider the opinion of other people and believe that whatever we do is the right thing. After all, it is difficult to be an adult all the time and by letting out the child in us, life becomes meaningful and worth living.

My father quite often told us a story of one of his bosses, who was very fond of dogs. He had an Alsatian, which was with him for almost fifteen years. Then, one day, it died and the professor was heartbroken. He could not bear to be separated from his dog. In the evening, he arranged for a funeral and invited his coterie of men. He had also arranged for a grave to be dug in the garden to bury his dog.

In the final hour, as he lifted his dog to place him in the grave, he became very upset and began to cry loudly. On seeing him sob, his beloved wife shedtears too and soon his friends also began to cry. And all this for a dog!

To an onlooker, the whole incident may seem funny and, perhaps, a bit too exaggerated but to the professor the dog meant a lot and he gave vent to his feeling in a childlike manner. And no one tried to stop him from acting in such a way.

Once, I had taken out my children to a trade fair. The children enjoyed riding the Ferris wheel, merry-go-round and the train, taking part in the duck ride and other wonderful games. They also enjoyed boating in the mini swimming pool and played on the bouncing bag jumping higher and higher until they fell back. How I yearned to join my kids!

Then we reached a particular spot marked THE STATUE MAN. Here, a man stood dressed like a statue and he did not even blink his eyelids. People gathered there made all sorts of funny faces and gestures and cracked jokes just to make him laugh, but in vain. Just as we were wondering whether this man was deaf, dumb and blind, for it was rather difficult to stand there motionless, without any reaction, the man jumped high up in the air scaring off all the people around and then within a second resumed his usual place.

Then as we moved on, we came across a game meant for children above twelve and so I told my children that they had to skip that one. It was a superfast merry-go-round and only meant for healthy and courageous people of the adventurous kind. Just then I saw an old nun around forty five years, go to the ticket counter and purchase a ticket for the ride. My legs refused to move further and along with my kids, I stood there watching what the old nun was up to.

This merry-go-round was a superfast one and it had about thirty swings hanging from a heavy metal circular ring. The swings were at a fairly good height from the ground and one had to jump high to sit comfortably on it. And if a person having high blood pressure ventured to take this ride, his BP was sure to shoot up. Even to the onlookers, it had a telling effect and our heads swirled watching the superfast merry-go-round.

The nun had probably come all alone to the trade fair as I could see no one near her. She showed her ticket and coolly vaulted on to one of the swings and made herself comfortable. When the guard finally switched on the button, the swings began to go round, at first slowly and then gradually picked up speed. Watching it, my head began to spin. The people taking the ride were undaunted and enjoyed it all the while screaming aloud. The nun had shut her eyes tightly and curled up her feet and gripping the chains of the swing tightly, was savouring this thrilling ride.

As I turned to leave the spot, I dwelt on the unusual behaviour of the nun. Nuns were expected to be in control of their emotions and not give into impulsive behaviour. How could she have acted in a childlike manner, unmindful of the decorum expected of a nun! I realised that I too had been childish enough to stop by with my children, just to watch the uncommon sight of a nun enjoying herself. In fact, I had also succumbed to the childish urge in me!

Well, all of us behave in childish ways at some point of time or the other. However, this indeed helps us to remove the boredom of our monotonous lives. For the most difficult thing on earth is to remain unmoved, like "The Statue Man" at the fair. He was doing it, as he was being paid for it. It is rather difficult to always be in perfect control of our emotions and feelings.

Of course, while we do have a certain amount of freedom to behave according to our whims and fancies, we should also be careful not to hurt others - for yielding to our urges at the cost of others is not the right thing to do!

Once, when my brother was preparing for his diploma, he was sent for training to a Plastic Manufacturing Unit. The middle-aged trainer's squeaky voice and mannerisms tickled his funny bone and my brother couldn't help grinning. Next the trainer took him to a giant machine and started explaining the minute details of the manufacturing process. All of a sudden my brother was overcome by a fit of laughter. Although he had tried hard to maintain a straight face, the gestures of the trainer and the gravity with which he explained the process, made him laugh aloud. The trainer did not mind him laughing and continued his lecture even more earnestly. My brother was unable to control his emotions and kept grinning all the while. The trainer did not say a word. Probably he must have been happy that his lecture had for once elicited laughter instead of boredom! Later in the evening, my brother was rather embarrassed by his peculiar behaviour.

Life is not something to be taken too seriously to be spent brooding all the time. Life is worth living and we must enjoy the pleasures it has to offer us! We should also relax with some fun and frolic. And once in a while, if the child in us wishes to prance, let us not try to suppress the urge! Our behaviour might excite laughter and soothe the much-troubled heart -for laughter is the best medicine !

12

On Speaking the Truth

Our Hindi teacher wore a gorgeous saree which enhanced her beauty and I sat, admiring her, throughout the class. She explained Mahatma Gandhi's concept of truth. Gandhiji adhered to truth all his life, so much so that he would not even lie to a small child. I don't know why, but this statement "not even lie to a child" registered in my impressionable mind. I was just eight years old then, studying in the fourth standard. From then on, I held the view that truth meant, not to lie even to a child. I decided that I should also follow in the footsteps of Mahatma Gandhi, sticking to truth all the time.

Even at that young age, I was aware of the fact that God is omnipresent, omnipotent and omniscient and that if we ever did a wrong, we were sure to be punished. This I learnt from my parents who were very God-fearing. So, if by chance, I spoke a lie or hurt anybody, while offering my prayers, I would confess my sins to Him and beg for His forgiveness.

Everything seemed quite fine until I reached the ninth standard. This was a very tough year for me because the teachers were putting us under continuous pressure and preparing us for the tenth standard public examinations. We had frequent tests and assignments and the teachers evaluated our papers strictly. Because of this, almost everyone, excepting a few brilliant students, scored average marks.

However, one day we learnt that the students of the other section were scoring better marks as compared to us. The reason one found out, was that they helped each other during the tests, hoodwinking the teachers adroitly by adopting various ploys. So the girls decided that we too had to share our knowledge during tests and score better marks. This way, we could at least please our worried parents and escape their constant nagging.

The class leader explained that the teachers were after all doing their job by giving us rigorous training and the public exam papers would not be as difficult as the ones that the teachers were setting for us. The justification given by the leader was convincing and all of us agreed to her request. Though I disliked the decision taken by them, I kept silent and didn't offer my opinion. I was rather too bashful to disclose my individual opinion. Moreover, I had no other option as the girls forced me to abide by their decision and when they asked whether I was willing, I meekly nodded my head as a mark of acceptance.

The next day, we had a science test and all of us were set to assist one another. In the afternoon, our science teacher entered the class with a sheet of paper and started writing the questions on the blackboard. The fourth question was very difficult and I put a small dash against it and dared not ask anybody for the answer. My partner, sitting beside me, asked me if I knew the answer to the fourth question and I shook my head, meaning I did not know. It was my bad luck that at that very instant, our science teacher who was daydreaming at the window, turned back and seeing me shake my head, thought I was discussing the answers.

She shouted out my name and commanded me to sit on the floor and do the test. I was terribly angry with my partner for putting me in this embarrassing position. I also felt ashamed for having been a party to their scheme.

I decided that cheating or copying was not for me. I was meant not to be a cheat and God had punished me enough. The next day at school, I told my friends that I would not be a party to their agreement and that I did not mind scoring low marks. Slowly, I stopped talking to my friends and preferred to be left all alone. During the recess and lunch hour, I spent my time preparing for the exams. I referred to guides and reference books and began taking notes.

New Year's Eve was fast approaching. This year was going to be the most memorable one in my life, for I was to appear for the public exams, that would in a way decide my fate for the rest of my life. Unless one enjoyed the grace of God, however much one strives, one is not much benefited. And so, besides studying very hard, I had to obtain the love and blessings of God. That year, on New Year's Day, I spent almost an hour, singing hymns and offering prayers in front of God, evoking His blessing for my public exams. In return for the same, I promised Him that I would adhere to truth all my life ; like Mahatma Gandhi I would never lie even to a child!

I took great care of what I said, so much so that I wished not to lie, even by a slip of my tongue. For this would elicit the wrath of God which would result in my getting tough question papers in the public examination.

Two months after I had taken the resolution, I was pleased that I had not spoken a single lie to any one. One fine day, as I dumped my heavy sack of books on my desk, I felt rather happy that I was able to keep my vow, and the fact that God too was aware of this made me even more happy for it meant an easy public exam - at least I believed it would be so.

After a heavy lunch, I sat at my desk, studying the previous notes. Just then the bell rang and our Hindi master entered the classroom, burping loudly. He had just been transferred from Uttar Pradesh and did not know a word of English. Throughout, he spoke in Hindi and was always threatening us that we were much below the mark. After his usual advice that we should work hard, he began teaching us a poem by Tulsidas.

He taught us extremely well, explaining the poem word by word. However, during the last ten minutes of the period, my concentration began to sag and my mind started planning how to spend the evening at home, what subjects I had to give preference to and whether the servant would have come home, else Mother would ask me to do the dishes - I was in a different world!

Then at last, the bell rang indicating the end of the period and I came back to my senses. The teacher was also happy that his class was over and he asked the class, if we understood the poem and looked around for a response. Happy that the Hindi class was over - because to me it was the most boring subject in which I always got low marks - I looked at the master, glad that he was going. The master's gaze met mine and now he repeated his question addressing me directly since he got no reply from the rest of the class.

As my mind was preoccupied during the last ten minutes, I had not understood the concluding paragraphs of the poem. How could I tell him the truth that I did not understand the last paragraph because I had not been concentrating, and that too in faltering Hindi. Being a shy person, I rarely spoke to anybody. Once, when a new teacher asked us to introduce ourselves, I had almost forgotten my name, when it was my turn to introduce myself. With great difficulty, I had found my voice, mumbled a few words and then sat down.

Now the Hindi master was determined to get an answer from me and I was rather confused whether to just nod my head or tell him the truth. Nodding my head, would mean I was speaking a lie and would be breaking my vow. For that very instant, God would know that I had spoken a lie! More than that, I did not want to hurt my own conscience! He was not going to let me off the hook and looking at me, he yelled for the third time, "It is you I am asking girl. Did you understand the poem or not?"

The silence was becoming very conspicuous and everyone's attention was focussed on me now. It was a do-or-die situation and I had no choice. My mouth became parched with fear and gathering all the courage I had, I blurted out in faltering Hindi that I had not understood the last stanza. Then, he started bawling at me. How would I tell him about my resolution of not speaking a lie, no matter what! Well! God was watching the whole show and now He would be very pleased that I had kept my vow! And He would also be watching the cruel Hindi teacher shout at an innocent girl for which he would have to pay later on!

He then asked my partner, if she had understood the poem and on getting an assurance from her, advised her to clarify my doubts.

That day, I indeed felt mortified at being made a laughing stock.But I also experienced an inner joy and a unique satisfaction for having spoken the truth. I also felt that I had been given VIP treatment by our strict Hindi master for he had singled me out and I had been the centre of attention for a few minutes that day.

After completing my studies and embarking on my career, things changed altogether! At the workplace, I had to get along with different kinds of people. Many of them were older than me and were quite experienced in life. Most of them liked my reserved nature, and shared their problems with me as I listened to them patiently. They were confident that I would not betray their trust to anybody. Besides, I learnt that people respected and loved you when you spoke to them with kindness and exhibited humility without much bragging and egotism.

Slowly with age and experience, I learnt that it was not the trait of truthfulness that really mattered as much as trying not to hurt the feelings of others. My views on saying the truth also underwent a sea change and I began practising avoiding the three A's of anger, arrogance and arguments in my conversations with people. This of course is very difficult and I am still trying my best to attain perfection!

Whenever I think of my teenage obsession with regard to speaking the truth, I feel deeply disconcerted. But I must thank God for having freed me from the sheer craziness of sticking to the truth and changing my views on it! Otherwise, when my children asked me why their photos were missing in the marriage album, I would have to get down to explaining the facts of life!

13

For Dog Lovers

After inspecting the house thoroughly, I was at last successful in finding a coconut shell without holes in it. Running into the kitchen, I asked mother to pour some milk into it and placed it in front of the frightened pup lying in a corner of the bedroom. The puppy lapped up the whole milk eagerly and then started wagging his tail, thanking me for the kind gesture.

It all began, when a stray dog gave birth to cute puppies in an abandoned hut. I begged mother to allow me carry home one of the puppies and keep it as a pet. Mother refused, telling me that it was very difficult for her to take care of five young children and a dog would be an additional burden on her. But I promised that the puppy would be my entire responsibility and all that she would have to do was spare some milk everyday, and hesitantly, mother agreed.

Thus started my affiliation with dogs when I was hardly nine years old. That night, I made up a bed for the puppy, inside our bedroom. I decided to sleep with the puppy and when I lay down by his side, I found it difficult to stretch out my legs comfortably. However, I did not complain and wished to continue sleeping with the pup. In the morning, when I woke up, I found that the puppy has stealthily left the place and was sleeping on the carpet near my siblings. Thereafter I let him sleep along with us. Though mother kept yelling that dogs were to be kept outside to watch the house, I did not pay heed to her.

My joy was short-lived for one fine day father informed us that our new house which he was building in another town nearby, was almost ready and we would be moving there. My heart broke at the thought of leaving my friend. However, father promised to get me another puppy after settling into our new residence. On the day we vacated our house, I left the puppy with a heavy heart.

On the very first day in our new residence, there was good news awaiting me! I was rather happy to learn that our neighbour's dog was pregnant. With time, the neighbours became our friends and as soon as their dog gave birth to puppies, I carried home a brown puppy and named him Jimmy. This puppy stayed with us for just two years. In spite of good care, the puppies of our neighbour's dog lived only for two to three years and succumbed to one form of disease or the other. In order to assuage the distress caused by the demise of the previous dogs, I made it a point to always select a brown colour pup and named all of them after Jimmy.

But once, it so happened that the dog gave birth to quadruplets and there was no brown puppy among them. I was in a fix and after pondering over it a great deal, I selected a cream-coloured puppy. Somehow I was not very satisfied with it and after a month decided to exchange him for a black one. I had heard people tell me that black dogs were good watchdogs and that they had sharp vision and could even detect ghosts in the air. I found the black puppy was rather disobedient and refused to obey my commands. He kept chasing the sparrows and cats and I realised that Blacky was a wild dog and wished to send him back. This way, both the dogs got a chance of staying with us for a month each, until one day, they took it upon themselves to return and refused to budge from our house, having decided to always remain together. My attempts to separate the dogs were in vain and this resulted in our having two dogs.

Though Jimmy had a gentle nature, very soon, he learnt all the dirty tricks from Blacky and started chasing chickens and birds. He would accompany Blacky everywhere and was out of the house the whole day and returned only at night. As time passed, both Jimmy and Blacky turned out to sturdy dogs and good hunters!

Everyday, mother received complaints from the neighbours that our dogs had killed their chickens or had bitten the goats. Mother was helpless and she was silent over this issue until one fine day, a lady came to our house along with the village headman. She complained that our dogs had killed one of her goats and so she wanted compensation for the same. Very soon many other women joined her and complained to the village headman about the atrocities committed by our dogs. After considering the matter at length, the headman gave the verdict that our dogs must be killed. They also promised to hire two gypsies to carry out the cruel act. We had no say in the matter!

On the appointed day, two gypsy men arrived with their big guns. All of us were away at school, and Mother was alone at home. After showing them our dogs, Mother shut the door behind her in anguish. Shortly the loud sound of shots being fired rent the air and Blacky fell dead with a long, loud yelp, followed by Jimmy. Their painful cries pierced my mother's heart and she was in agony the whole day. In the evening, she recounted the sad story of how the dogs were shot and also told us that we should stop rearing dogs henceforth. I agreed to her request.

Months elapsed and I missed my friends! Early every morning, I was reminded of how the dogs would run towards me and enjoy being petted. Sometimes, I would share my grief with them shedding copious tears into their rough coats, and they would listen to everything, as though they understood whatever I said. At times, I would also give vent to my anger by beating them harshly for some petty mischief they had committed. Later on, I would compensate for my harshness with an excessive display of love. Whenever I returned home, they would pounce on me expressing their pleasure in seeing me back. Now, I missed them miserably!

A year passed by and very soon our neighbour's dog passed away too. Hence, I forgot all about dogs for quite some time. But early one morning, I woke up to the sound of people shouting outside, and the reason I learnt was that a thief had stolen our brand new bicycle. It was then, that my parents felt the absence of dogs!

Once again, I was bent on having dogs! While returning from my workplace one day, I saw a cute Alsatian puppy strolling about in the midst of the slums. That night, I had a talk with my brothers and told them to pick up the puppy, after seeking permission from the people living there. One of my brothers scolded me for not having given up on rearing dogs. He yelled that at an age when I should be raising kids, I was still looking for puppies and that it was a matter of great shame! But I wanted the puppy, no matter what. The next day, the puppy was there at home. Of all the puppies I had come across, this was the most beautiful one and how much joy it gave me!

It was Sunday morning and all of us were deeply engrossed in a TV serial. When the programme was over, I came out to spend away some time with my pet and called out his name.

There was no response and I shouted out even louder and still Jimmy was nowhere to be found. I became mad with anxiety and darted from one place to another searching for him. A boy standing outside, informed us that the puppy had been standing near the gate wagging his tail and when a passer-by had called out to him, the puppy had coolly squeezed himself through the gate and followed the man. The man had picked up the pup and disappeared in a jiffy. My heart broke and very soon I sent my brothers and father in quest of the lost dog.

My brothers returned empty-handed and I eagerly waited for my father to bring some good news. When Father returned after an hour - which seemed likes ages to me - he told me that one of his friends had promised to give him another sturdy dog and that our puppy was not traceable.

It was already twilight and the sounds of "Allah-o-Akbar" blared from the nearby mosque. Immediately an idea struck me. The mosque generally made small announcements now and then about a missing child, or a person who was lost, or about the arrival of the water tankers informing people to fetch water from there. I pleaded with father to arrange for such an announcement to be made about our missing dog.

Being the first child in the family, I enjoyed the love and respect of my parents, especially my father's, so much so that whenever I was in distress, my father would get very perturbed. He couldn't bear to see me hurt in any way. Though he knew that my request was hare-brained, he left reluctantly for the mosque just to please me. But his proposal was turned down curtly. That was the end of my association with dogs!

Very soon, my marriage was settled and I forgot all about dogs! Married life was altogether a different kind of experience. I was busy getting to know each and every one in my new family and had absolutely no time for dogs. But someday, I hope to renew my association with them - probably, when I am old enough and my children are grown and have their own problems to bother about and when my husband stops strutting around me to see what is cooking and leaves me alone. I plan to have a dog then, and enjoy its pure love and affection. For there can be no truer friend and companion like a dog who gives us unconditional joy!

14

My Tutors

My parents were childless for eight long years after their marriage. Then one fine day, God answered their prayers and I was born to them. Anything obtained after much hardship and difficulty is worth its weight in gold and so was I to my parents. I gave them all the joy and happiness that they yearned for. Just two years later, my mother was pregnant again and this time, they wished to have a boy. But their desire was not fulfilled and my sister was born. My father became very depressed. However, he did not get bogged down by this fact and instead wished to turn it into an opportunity. It was then that he took a major decision in his life. He was determined to bring me up like a boy - to give me the best education, to enable me to secure a good job and lead an independent life. My father had taken a very brave decision, for he was born and brought up in a family where girls were looked down upon and kept indoors and were expected to be proficient in housework and were not even sent to school.

He got me admitted to the best convent school. Everyday, he took me to school and hired a man to pick me up in the evenings. When he dropped me to school, he made it a point to meet the teacher and find out how I was faring. Gradually he came to know her well enough to request her to give some extra coaching to me at home, to which she readily agreed. Once again, in the evenings he would come home early and take me on his bicycle to my teacher's house, which was quite far away from home. While I learnt the alphabet and numbers, my father did the shopping and returned within an hour to collect me. And when I came out, he would treat me to biscuits and bananas. Fierce storms or heavy rains did not once hinder him from this ritual.

My teacher was an Anglo-Indian and she always wore a tight-fitting frock that came up to her knees and had short hair. There was a servant, who lived with her and as I entered the gate, I would see him cleaning the long fishes to cook for dinner. I would go in grimacing, detesting the smell of fish. The old lady made me feel at home and was always full of appreciation for me. One evening, she gifted me with a sharpener and a chocolate for doing my lessons so well and my joy knew no bounds. I felt on top of the world and ran about displaying it to all and sundry with pride.

The next year, I had a different teacher for UKG. The teacher was a rigid woman. Everyday, in the afternoons, the ayahs would spread out a long bed sheet and we children would be asked to lie down and go to sleep. Most of the days, I would not be able to sleep and would pretend to do so by closing my eyes tightly, for all those who were awake, were given a sharp lash on the buttocks. Fear generally hinders growth and so I was rather scared of my teacher and ultimately this was reflected in my results. One fine day, the grumpy headmistress called my father and told him harshly that I was not doing well in studies and hence would have to be retained another year. My father was furious with the way the headmistress had dealt with the matter. He had more confidence in me than in the teacher. Immediately without saying a word, he requested for a transfer certificate. He coached me well at home and admitted me directly to the first standard in a Central School.

That was when the whole problem started. For in the Central School, the medium of instruction was Hindi of which my father had no idea. Since he could not teach me Hindi, he was forced to send me out for tuitions. He met my Hindi teacher and requested her to tutor me at her residence. The Hindi teacher was a Malayalee and was fair and stout. She had two small children to take care of and hence was always busy at home. She would give me enough writing work and attend to her cooking. On some days, when she was sick, she would lie down in bed and ask me to wake her up once her husband returned from office. The moment I informed her about her husband's arrival, she would leap out of the bed and get into the kitchen and get busy with her work. After setting the question paper for the examinations, she would rehearse all the important questions with me. Sometimes, if she happened to be the invigilator, she would peep into my paper and guide me too.

I regularly attended her tuitions for almost two years. Now, it was time for my sister to attend an interview for admission to the first standard. My father drilled her at home night and day and on the day of the interview he took her to school neatly dressed, with a notebook in her hand. Once she was called inside, she was so scared that she did not open her mouth and whatever questions they put to her, she remained mum and did not reply. It so happened that my Hindi teacher happened to be there and seeing a notebook in her hand, asked her to at least write down the alphabet. It was then that she saw my name written on top of the notebook and also the Hindi notes which she had taught me. Immediately, my sister was given admission.

When I reached the third standard, my Hindi teacher changed and so did my tutor. But things changed, when I reached the fourth standard. Father was burdened with the responsibility of taking care of a large family - for my three brothers were born in quick succession, with a gap of one year each. He could not devote much time to me by taking me all the way to the residence of my tutors. Thus he decided to arrange for a tutor to come home.

He requested his office watchman, who was from the North, to inform him about anyone who could come home and teach me Hindi. The watchman volunteered that his mother tongue was Hindi and that he was also an educated person and was prepared to coach me in the evenings. My father struck a deal with him and I had a Hindi tutor at home who looked like an army man. Very soon, I found out that his demeanour as well his nature was very harsh and he did not possess a soft heart. I was scared stiff of him.

One evening, I was playing outside, when I saw my Hindi tutor riding his bicycle towards our house. Even after seeing him, I continued with my game, waiting for him to summon me. He did call me but warned me that at the time of his arrival, he wished to see me reading at the table and not playing outside. He always scolded me for each and every mistake I made and I became even more frightened of him. Some days, when I could not resist the temptation, I would go out and play and on spying my tutor far off, I would flee inside and pretend to be reading.

Since my father had no time to teach me, I was doing very badly in other subjects as well, but I did not realise the seriousness of that. One day, my Hindi tutor told me that scolding me had had no effect and he was going to use the rod. The next day, he came with a thin rod and threatened to spank me with it if I did not study well. The very sight of him created panic in me and I would cry whenever he scolded me.

One day, while he was teaching me a new lesson, mother summoned me to have coffee and I ran into the kitchen. After having mine, I brought another cup of coffee and placed it in front of the teacher. Instead of thanking me, he became very furious and shouted at me for lacking in manners for running away into the kitchen, without seeking his permission. He made me stand for the remaining hour as punishment. This was the last straw and that evening, after he left, I sobbed and conveyed to my mother my feelings of fear and hatred of studying under this tough master. I assured her that I would study well all by myself.

In fact, I had been pleading with mother from the very first day the Hindi tutor had stepped into our house. But Mother had been putting off my request under one pretext or the other. She would tell me that, since father had found him with great difficulty, it was my duty to put up with everything and study well without complaining. Everyday, I would brief my mother of his atrocities and she would simply brush aside my blabber, saying that she would talk to father about it.But on this particular day, when I told her about him shouting at me for having my coffee, she took it a bit seriously. She was rather moved and promised to help me out. In return, she put forth some conditions which I was to abide by. I was to help her out and do the petty jobs she assigned me from time to time without grumbling and also had to take care of my little brother and never let him cry. I readily accepted both her conditions and jumped about in great excitement.

Mother did talk it out with father and the following month I was relieved from the "terrorist's" visits in the evenings. I was free as a bird and obeyed mother and was of great help to her in return for her kind gesture. I did everything for mother but did not study and failed to understand the gravity of not doing well at school. That year I failed! father was deeply worried about my future. He tried hard not to express his grief and instead advised me not to worry and said that I would do well the next year if I studied. How much my failure had affected him, I learnt a few days later, for he stopped wearing the red vermilion mark on his forehead as a matter of habit after offering prayers to God, before leaving the house.

How true it is that failures are the stepping stones to success ! My failure had brought about a change in me. It was due to the fact that father remained silent over my failure and pacified me by telling that he was confident, that I would do better the next year. I wanted to make Father happy and proud of me. I also understood the reality that Father would be happy only if I studied and scored high marks in all subjects. I began to study in earnest. I made friends with students who scored very high marks and cleared my doubts with them. There was such a vast improvement in my studies that one teacher asked who was coaching me at home and I told her proudly that I had learnt everything by myself. From then on, there was no looking back, and I passed all my examinations with above average marks and fulfilled the dreams of my father. Besides that, the strong foundations that father had laid when he tutored me also helped me train all my siblings at home itself.

Today, I don't send my children for tuitions. Though the tutors might indeed be of some help, I strongly believe that there is nothing like training them to be self-starters. Spoon-feeding may prove helpful in the initial stages, but as children grow, one should enable them to learn things on their own without constant interference. After a particular stage, one must stop spoon-feeding and pampering them as this only hampers their progress. I wish to let my children develop on their own by setting their own aims and goals and achieving them one after another by dint of hard labour and perseverance. In fact, I don't like to rob them of the joy one experiences when one's dreams come true by simply working very hard, putting one's heart and soul into it, be it anything. They will learn the lessons of life all by themselves, for experience is the best teacher!

15

My First Job

As the light blue van headed towards the gate, I inserted a sheet of paper into the typing machine and kept the matter to be typed out close at hand. In a few minutes, the doctor stormed into the large library hall, and as he crossed my table, I wished him "good morning" and sat down to continue my work. In the centre of the hall was a large table on which was placed the morning newspapers. As he browsed through the pages, I slowly began clicking on my typewriter, glad that I had some work on hand. For, as doctor left the hall, he would stop near my table and interrogate me as to what I was doing and I would try to impress him by making a show of how busy I was!

This was my first job and I was filled with fear that if I did not seem to have enough work to do, I would either be dumped with extra work or be sent home. I worked here as a stenotypist and also had to take care of the small library. I was fresh out of school and hardly eighteen years old and to me, this place was more or less like another school.

It was a small research laboratory with young scientists who had experience in different fields. The director of this organisation was a sixty-year-old man, a retired professor from a reputed institute.He was always dressed in white and his hair was silvery grey. He was lovingly called Doc, by everyone on the campus. He was the founder of this institute and many of the young scientists were his own students. Despite his age he was very energetic. His office was on the second floor of the lab and had no proper staircase. It was reached by climbing an iron ladder. While writing his reports, he wished to be free from disturbance and hence had no phone in his office.

Probably, because of his age or his profession as a teacher, he always spoke loudly. His voice could be heard throughout the campus. He had a bad temper and kept bawling at each and everyone who passed his way and I was very scared of him.

But Doc had a soft heart too! For, in the days, when people were looking for experienced hands, he gave a job to a beginner like me, who had absolutely no work experience. He was of the opinion that unless people were given jobs, how would they learn. And his sole aim in founding the research laboratory was to be able to reach out to the poor. All the scientists were working on projects based on low-cost technology, and Doc made the technology available to the poor people.

I myself had a great interest in science and wished to continue my studies in college. But father was against sending me to college and he got me a job through the recommendation of his friend, an old student of Doc's. Hence, I enrolled myself in the university's correspondence course and started studying English Literature. Being in the midst of scientists, I felt very inferior and thought that I could have also been a scientist, had I continued my studies. However, very soon, I realised that no college would have taught me what I learnt in this organisation.

Since all the scientists gave their notes and research findings to me for typing, I gained knowledge in different subjects.

I learnt about windmills, about the process of manufacturing shampoos from wood ash, about using Gonkura leaves as a substitute for tamarind, about plastic catamarans for the poor fishermen, about spirulina proteins, about solar energy and about all the "bio's" - biogas, biomass, bioclock and biotechnology and what not! Once, in a while, Doc gave lecturers on various topics and I was also invited to join the team.

One day, a young lady - a ravishing beauty - entered the hall and sat in the library. While I sat admiring her, Doc came in and began to discuss the project she was to commence working on. He was carrying out an extensive study on the tribal people living in the Kumaon Hills in the Himalayan Range. After their meeting was over, she requested me to do some typing for her and I readily agreed to do it. It was her resume and while typing it out I learnt that she was the daughter of my old school principal. Thrilled, I jumped up and introduced myself as her mother's student. She was herself happy to know about it and promised to tell her mother.

A few weeks later, she came along with her mother, my old principal, and my heart began to beat rapidly on seeing her. As she stepped into the hall, I stood up and flashed a broad smile at her. After a small chat with me, she requested me to continue working. While she waited for Doc, she enquired if I was happy with my job. Just then, Doc entered and with a broad smile she told him that I was her student. It was a proud moment in my life!

One day, Doc gave me a slip of paper with an address scribbled on it and asked me to type the same on an envelope. His handwriting was hard to decipher ; however, I managed to type out what I could make of it. When I handed it over to him, he frowned fiercely and I braced myself for a blast from him. He shouted at me for writing the wrong PIN code. When he screamed at me in front of so many people, I felt very awkward standing there like an idiot. Suddenly, my adrenaline shot up and I retorted sharply that it was the PIN code that was given to me and it was not my mistake. His anger now rose sky high and even before I could complete my sentence, he yelled, "don't you try to argue with me like that!" The noise made everyone turn around and stare at me. He continued shouting, "First learn to accept your mistakes and stop arguing !" I realised that nothing I said would make any difference and decided that, that was the end of everything. From then on, I was not even going to look at Doc's face. I made up my mind that very soon, I would have to leave the place as I could not tolerate his frequent and loud rebukes, in front of everyone, that too when I was an innocent and soft-spoken young girl!

The next day, as soon as he entered the library, he came to me and asked me in a low and kind tone, "are you fine sweetheart ? Is everything okay ?" And I lied to him that I was feeling fine. Somehow, after that incident I never dared to argue with Doc. Whenever he bawled at me I would remain silent, even when I knew I was right.

Gradually, this became a habit with me, so much so, that whenever anybody rebuked me, I would try not to retort and remained silent - for Doc's words "don't argue" still kept ringing in my mind. This is the place, where I learnt that the best way to tackle an argument is to avoid it in the first place. This has of course stood me in good stead in later life.

Once a senior lady scientist wanted a particular book. After searching the racks thoroughly, I informed her that it was not available. She then told me to purchase the same from a book store, as she required it for some urgent reference work. I stood there open-mouthed, as though she had asked me to go to the United States, that too all alone! What the hell was she thinking? How dare she ask me - a teenage girl - to go all alone and buy a book? Did she not know that girls were not allowed to go out alone ? Though this office a just a fifteen minutes' walk from my house, one of my brothers drops me everyday and picks me up from here. I was brought up with love and care by my parents, and my father alway accompanied me wherever I went and by me everything I needed, and how dare this old lady ask me to go out all alone ? Surely, she must be insane ! When she repeated the question again, I meekly shook my head and she blustered, "why the hell do you people come out to work ? I did not answer, for my experience had taught me never to argue, especially with the oldies.

I was brought up in a very peculiar manner. My father would not even let me walk on my own in front of the house. He did not like me standing near the gate or chatting with neighbours . The only freedom I had was to go to school. I was repeatedly advised by mother that good girls don't talk to people on the road and they always walk with their heads bent low. They don't talk or laugh aloud in a manner that causes others to turn back and stare. Having grown in such an atmosphere, I hardly knew which bus to board to reach a particular destination or in which shop to buy what. In a nutshell, I was like a frog in a deep well!

It was only after marriage, that I was able to climb out of this well! My husband was quite different and did not approve of my reserved nature. He wished that I speak in a candid manner and wear modern clothes. He took me out to big hotels and family functions quite often and the shy and self-conscious feeling which shrouded me gradually left me. My frequent shopping sprees also taught me about where a particular product could be found and today, I go out shopping all alone without any feelings of shyness or fear. He gave me independence and trusted me and I slowly came out of my shell and proved myself a confident being!

But at times, when we have our fights, and I try to boss over him, he reminds me of the past, and the naïve person that I had been and how he was the one to transform me. And immediately, one particular incident would come to my mind.

It was just a week after our marriage. My husband had stopped his motorbike in front of a store and handed me a ten-rupee note asking me to buy potato chips. My heart began to beat faster and I was able to hear its pounding. If I told him that I had no experience in shopping and that my father accompanied me everywhere, I was afraid he would consider me an idiot, an innocent village girl, fit for nothing. He would then start berating my parents for the way they had sheltered me and this would immediately get on my nerves and a big fight would ensue. I wisely wanted to avoid a confrontation - at least not on the street. I was now between the devil and the deep sea and having no choice, I grabbed the ten-rupee note, and started walking towards the store.

I had no idea what to ask the shopkeeper, for I knew nothing about weights and quantities. Would 100 gm of chips be too large an amount! Or would the shopkeeper laugh at me for asking for such a small quantity. On reaching the counter, I handed over the note to the man sitting there and demanded potato chips for rupees ten. After studying me for a while, he enquired, "shall I give you 1/4 kg for rupees eleven?" I nodded happily and the man turned back and pulled out a very big plastic packet and began stuffing potato chips into it.

While my hubby was waiting impatiently for me, wondering what the hell was going on, I ran to him as though I had won an Olympic gold medal, and asked for a one-rupee coin. He then said, "I asked you to buy chips for just the two of us and not for the whole family!" And I bluffed that it was my favourite snack. Two weeks later, when my understanding of him grew better, I confessed the whole thing to him and he had a hearty laugh listening to my story.

Today if, I am a confident person, comfortable with my self and others, I owe it to my first job and I will always be grateful to Doc, for he had been the one who helped me take the first mighty step - by giving me a job and teaching me all about working in an organisation. With the experience gained, I was easily able to switch from one job to another until I got the best job of my choice and was settled in life!

16

The KBC Issue

Even when I was in class eight, my father would bring home copies of the *Reader's Digest*, a well-renowned monthly magazine, from his office library and ask me to go through it, during my leisure time. Though, I could not understand the meaning of each and every word, I would read all the articles and get a gist of it. Once again, during the vacations, he would advice me not to sit idle, but to read the newspaper fully, especially the editorial column, to develop my English vocabulary and also to keep abreast of things happening around the world. I would earnestly sit down with a dictionary and read the whole newspaper which would take me about half the day!

I had wondered then why Father had instructed only me to spend my time thus, and not my other siblings. Today, I know the answer to that! It is because, they would have hardly cared to listen to him! For even today, when I am middle-aged, I look forward to his advice on trivial matters like whether I should send my daughter for the school excursion or not; and I am made fun of for being so childish and dependent. But then, I have grown up with such love and pampering that I am unable to break free from those ties!

One day, I am going to be old too, and what joy it would bring me if my son or daughter confered with me on all matters and held me in high esteem! And I pride myself for having given my parents that unique pleasure. But the advice my father gave me one find day, turned my life topsy-turvy for a brief period of time!

It was 9 P.M. when he rang up and as I lifted the phone, he said, "There is an interesting quiz programme on TV, hosted by the famous Hindi actor Amitabh Bachchan. The questions are so simple and with your excellent general knowledge, you can give it a try!"

The programme he referred to was *Kaun Banega Crorepati* (KBC). The quiz game show had fifteen multiple choice questions, and the one who answered them all correctly was to be rewarded with a cash prize of Rs. one crore! Of course one had also the benefit of three lifelines to seek help from, when one was not sure of the answer. Well, once again it was money that Father was after. I told him that I really did not have the time for it and I was not interested.

However, he kept reminding me about the programme quite often and urged me to give it a try. One day, I went to my parents' home with my children and husband. After spending some time with us, Father went inside saying he had got a gift for me. He returned with a small package inside which was a quiz book meant specially for the KBC programme. I just scanned through the pages and suddenly my interest in the programme was aroused. I decided to give it a try for a trial costs nothing. Thus began a mega project!

I talked it over with my husband and convinced him that if I had to take part in the KBC show, his cooperation was the most important thing. First of all he would have to let me watch the programme from 9 P.M. to 10 P.M. everyday. He should also let me prepare for it, without grumbling. He gave his consent immediately! I then assured him that, I would pray to God whole-heartedly and try my best to win the Rs. one crore-prize money, which he could spend as he liked. My husband was quick to interrupt, "Thirty per cent of that will have to be given as tax !" And I told him that seventy lakhs was not a small amount either.

I would first of all take my family on a world tour! I would travel by executive class and sit amidst rich businessmen, famous actors and reputed politicians! Looking at me, they would first wonder as to who this ordinary woman was.Slowly my face would appear a little familiar. Then they would recall everything. Yes! This was the intelligent woman, who answered all the questions on the Big B's game show! And they would think how true it is that beauty and brains don't always go together. Ver soon they would all start staring at me and wish to have a conversation with me. Oh! God, at that time, please make me feel humble and do not let pride or ego take over me!

The summer vacations had begun and I was spared from school work. Having time on my hands, I decided to take the plunge. The preparations began in earnest. My mind was always preoccupied with what I had to read and what reference books I had to buy. One morning, while going up to my office, I was so engrossed in my study plan, that I continued climbing till the fourth floor. When I realised my mistake, I turned back and walked down to the third floor, where my office was. I felt like a schoolgirl once again filled with dread – as though everything depended on my passing the exam!

I purchased a general knowledge book for rupees twenty from a bookstall at the railway station followed by a hefty *Competition Success Review*. Then, I jotted down important points from it. I requested father to buy some more quiz books and very soon the table was piled high with reference books. I had almost spent thousand rupees towards the purchase of quiz books by various authors. I worried such a lot that I had very little time to prepare and felt that had I been a housewife, things would have been much easier !

I watched the quiz programme and found that the pattern of questions varied everyday and that they were on the basis the background of the participant who was sitting on the "hot seat"; his qualifications, nature of work, the politics and history of the place to which he belonged, his religion, language, culture and so on.

Hence, I subscribed to the magazine, *India Today* to have a fair knowledge of Indian politics. From the library, I borrowed the historical and religious comics, and read them over and over again. One day, I picked up about ten comics, and the librarian stared at me in great awe. I told him that I was taking it for some reference study and would return them within two days. I did not want to brag to him that it was for the KBC show, and wished to keep it a secret. *When he watches me on the TV quiz programme he will probably think, well it was for this, that the lady had taken all the books that day!*

My hands hurt as I jotted down the points from each and every reference book in front of me. Finally, the notes I gleaned almost became another thick book! I also realised that whatever I crammed from these books, I forgot the next instant. Preparing for the show was becoming too much of a bother and I was also filled with confusion of what exactly I ought to do. Then it occurred to me that my own preparations were not going to be helpful and God's blessing was all that mattered. I wrote the names of all the quiz books on different bits of paper and shuffled them in front of God. I then prayed to Him, "Oh God! Only you are aware of all the questions that I will be asked on the game show. Now, tell me the one and only book from this lot, which will help me achieve my goal!" Closing my eyes, I picked up a chit and to my astonishment, it was the very first book which I had purchased from the railway bookstall for just rupees twenty. Had I known it before, I could have avoided buying the other books and saved a lot of money!

The next day, I wrapped up all the quiz books together and placed them on a glass bookshelf. But whenever I went past the bookshelf I felt rather guilty. I had spent so much on these books and now they were gathering dust! However, I had taken a firm stand and didn't wish to muddle through these books again. I pulled out the package from the bookshelf and hurled it as far as I could into the loft where it would not be visible and from where it could not be easily brought down. I consoled myself that one day these books might be useful to my children and it was not a sheer waste of money, after all!

Day in and day out, I crammed the questions from the one and only quiz book selected by Him. Very soon, I was familiar with almost all the questions in it ! Everyday, I would sit on the floor with a notebook and pen and jot down the questions appearing on the game show. My children were too excited to even watch the programme! Not that they understood anything, but they were happy to see how animated their mom got when she knew the answer to one of the questions. Also, they were thrilled to see their mother sit in one place for such a long time. My daughter would prop herself against me and my three-year-old son would lie on my lap, enjoying the closeness.

One fine day, Big B announced that the phone lines were all open and the participants who wished to take part in the game show could try their luck.

Yes! I am going to try this time! Here I come, Mr Big B, to shake your hand and accompany you to the hot seat! I noted with diffidence that Mr B shook hands with women too (instead of saying namaskar, the usual Indian way of greeting others, by folding, the palms together). I would have to be courageous enough to shake hands with Big B! So, I was bent upon transforming my style and personality altogether. That weekend I went to a beauty parlour and got a U-shape haircut. *On seeing me in the game show, the beautician will tell her assistant proudly, "This was the lady who came to our parlour a few weeks back!"*

I dialled the number till my hands ached and finally left the task to my daughter. She sat by the phone and patiently tried the number continuously. Within a few minutes she succeeded and I ran over to the phone, with my heart pounding. A recorded voice said that I would first have to answer a multiple-choice question. Having not got over the excitement of getting the line, the question was neither audible nor clear to me. However, after evoking God's grace, I punched the answer. To my astonishment, the recorded voice said, "well done, your answer is right! Please stay by your phone on the 18th, and we will let you know if you are one of the lucky participants. And if for some reason you are not available on that day, we will move on to the next lucky contestant."

That night, while watching the programme, I became restless. One participant had answered all the fourteen questions correctly. He had to answer one more question to win the jackpot. Meanwhile, Big B was asking him what he intended to do with such a large sum. And the participant started bragging about his intentions. Suddenly, my imagination soared very high.

"Hemji, could you please tell us what you intend to do with your prize money?"

"Well, actually it was my father, who coaxed me into taking part in this programme and I would like to redeem his mortgaged house, and one of my brothers has got stranded in a foreign

land and I would like to help him come back and my sister....." and the Big B would cut in sharply, "let us continue after a short commercial break", for the list was going to be endless!

On D-Day I pulled up a chair and sat down, beside the phone. The recorded voice had warned, "if you are not available on that day, we will move on to the next lucky contestant". So I made it a point to stay close to the phone all day. It was just before noon when all of a sudden, I felt like going to the toilet, but quickly changed my mind. What if the expected call came at that point of time, when I was answering nature's call! I continued with my studies and waited in vain, up to 6 P.M. When the call didn't come through by then, I was completely dejected.

But there was always a second chance and I tried the line once again, and this time too, I did not get selected. It was then that I lost all hope and my instinct warned me that the KBC show was a wild goose chase! For, to be a participant on this game show, what mattered was a great deal of luck and not just hard work. Thereafter, I did not wish to waste my time on an enterprise which depended primarily on chance. I would rather slog over some befitting venture, where hard work really brought its own fruits. My children's vacations had also come to an end, and once again there was a cartload of homework and monthly tests which I had to attend to. I resolved the KBC issue by covering the TV with a large cover, vowing never to open it again for a very long time.

The story which I had heard numerous times from father came to my mind. Once, he had to work in the midst of a tribal community of Madhya Pradesh, in the late 1950s. The tribals had a very strange practice! When any member of the family passed away, they buried the corpse at the top of a mountain. After this, all the members of the family got together and rolled a huge rock from the foot of the hill to the summit and placed it near the spot of the burial. The size of the rock indicated the status of the family. A very huge and gigantic rock, signified an affluent family, with a lot of clout and power over people, which is why, they were able to push the rock, all the way up to the top of the mountain. The ignorant tribals did this just for fame and recognition! On careful speculation, I somehow felt that my struggles so far, for a similar end, were also as foolish.

My mind was plagued with different questions. What was I really after? Was it money? Or was is fame? Did I not know that both money and fame are evanescent and detrimental! They give us momentary joy and very slowly we start repenting as to why we acquired them in the first place. For these, have there own pitfalls, into which we would be ultimately drawn! With fame, we would lose our freedom to move around. It would also further result in our desire to be on top of the world! There is nothing that gives one more joy than a simple life, to be one among the crowd, unnoticed and preoccupied with one's own thoughts and ideas.

And did I not know that money ruined the mind, developing the desire to acquire more and more materialistic things. It would drive us with the urge to possess the entire world. A lot of money could make one lose the charm of living itself, for one would have everything in life. Life would become dull and drab! There is nothing like being in need of something and working hard to earn it! In fact, money could deprive one from enjoying the simple pleasures of life.

I had indeed arrived at an understanding about the futility of superfluous money and fame! But even after this incident, the desire to do something useful, be it a simple or a tiny act, which would bring happiness to others was kindled within me. This book is a result of that desire.

Index

Y